10-31
A *Halloween* Movie
Trivia Book

Gene DeRosa

10-31 A Halloween Movie Trivia Book

www.samsonpublishingcompany.com

Samson
Publishing
Company LLC

ISBN-13: 978-0692444474
ISBN-10: 0692444475

FIRST EDITION

DEDICATION

To my editor, my incredible wife, Traci, who over the past two
years has learned more about the *Friday the 13th* and *Halloween* films
than most die-hard horror fans know...
and she HATES horror and cannot watch it at all!

CONTENTS

ACKNOWLEDGMENTS

Thanks to:

John Carpenter and Debra Hill for creating something so good that it has grown and lasted many decades now, and has spawned so many great copies as well.

All of my fans, and yes, it still seems crazy to me that I can use that phrase. So many people have had kind words about my *Friday the 13*[th] book since it was released in the middle of 2014. One of the most important things for an author is word of mouth, and people have shared my work with friends and even strangers. I have met great people through this process and appreciate every one of them that has helped spread the word, offered great conversation, or even just a few encouraging words.

Once again to all my trivia friends who have sat around in a chat room with me every week for the better part of two decades now.

Diogo Landô, who did another great cover design this time around. Thank you again for being so easy to work with and for bringing visions from idea to amazing finished work.

Kevin S. King, who didn't just submit the fan questions you will see in the coming pages, but was also a great help in some of the research for things like the comic book and masks categories. He also helped by providing some of the photos you will see in the book, as well as finding someone to provide some of the photos he didn't have.

To the many cast members from the *Friday the 13th* movie franchise who I can now call associates and friends. You guys have opened up a whole new and exciting side of things for me and I do appreciate that opportunity.

Victor Miller, one of the aforementioned *Friday the 13th* cast members… not just ANY cast member, but the man who wrote and co-created the original film. It was amazing to hear his kind words about my book. It was a huge boost for me with it coming from the man that started it all. He also let me ask him a few questions to be used in this book as well. Thanks for the support, and I look forward to working together even more in the future.

Brooksanne Cline, who is a friend some of you may have heard me talk about before. She is the one that I was going to do the *M*A*S*H* trivia book with, but since she couldn't at that time, I did the *Friday the 13th* and now this *Halloween* book first. This time around, she was a big help with some research as well as letting me bounce ideas and questions off of her to see what she thought. Someday soon we will get that *M*A*S*H* book done!

Finally, thank you to my best friend, wife, and terrific editor, Traci! Without her, you would be about to read a jumbled mess of trivia questions. Thanks to her, though, it should all make sense to the masses. If you happen to see her sitting behind a table at a convention with me, you might tell her thank you yourself.

A NOTE FROM THE AUTHOR

I have to be honest. Growing up I wasn't a HUGE *Halloween* (the movies) fan. I watched them, and kind of liked them, but I was never fanatical about them like I was with *Friday the 13th* or *The Texas Chainsaw Massacre*. I don't really know why. Friends and I watched a lot of horror films through the years – many of which were bad.

What makes it even stranger is that I was a fan of many other John Carpenter films. The first horror film that I ever got to watch in a movie theater was actually John Carpenter's *The Thing*. One of my brothers and his long-time girlfriend (future wife) took me to the local one-screen theater to see it one night. It was a very small theater, which always made it an amazing experience to see any movie there – films like *Firefox*, *Missing in Action*, and even the very first film my mom ever dragged me to a few years prior to that night, *Coal Miner's Daughter*. Watching *The Thing* in this long and narrow single screen theater with amazing acoustics was a bit of an overwhelming experience for a twelve or thirteen year old. However, just like my first experience with horror (*Friday the 13th*) at the age of 9 (one month shy of 10), I got over the fear and absolutely loved it. This of course led me to watch more Kurt Russell and John Carpenter films. To this day I would probably say that *The Thing* is still my favorite from the Master of Horror.

I am very happy to say that the process of writing this book has made me rediscover the *Halloween* movie franchise and realize just how good they are. I had a similar experience while writing the *Friday the 13th* book, but with that I knew going in I really liked the series, and then realized that every one of the films had many reasons to like them (yes, even Parts 5 and 9 and *Jason X*). I now know that I actually do really love all of the films in the *Halloween* franchise as well. Some I like more than others of course, but they all have given me reasons to like them.

So many *Halloween* fans will say they despise Part 3, *The Curse of Michael Myers*, *Resurrection*, or even the Rob Zombie remakes. I also hate how when someone says they like one of those films, someone else says that the person is wrong for liking them. I think you are wrong if you DON'T like them. Sure, the original and Part Two are probably head and shoulders above the rest of the sequels and remakes, but each film gives you many reasons to like them. Personally, I might even say that Parts Four and Five are my favorites. I think it is mainly due to Danielle Harris's portrayal of Jamie Lloyd. It is amazing to me that she could express so much terror at such a young age, not to mention the fact that she didn't speak for the better portion of Part Five. I also love the remakes. One of the best parts of them to me is the back story of young Michael and Daeg Faerch's portrayal of the young psychopath. Part Two was way too Zombie-fied, but I still really liked it. Also, the most terrifying moment of the entire franchise comes in that Part Two remake. Annie's death scene is just so great. I love how at first we only hear it and then later get to see it in flashes of activity. I know many will agree with me when I say just like my favorite horror film, *The Texas Chainsaw Massacre*, sometimes the most terrifying things are the things implied that you don't really see. It is what makes the original *Chainsaw* and Annie's death scene so tremendous and horrifying.

As for *Halloween III*, I have to tell you that during this whole process, I have come across just as many people that love this film as I have that absolutely hate it. While it is not the traditional *Halloween*/Michael Myers film, it is a great standalone film – a bit strange, but still pretty good. You also need to realize that at the time, the plan was to end the Michael Myers storyline after Part Two and start an anthology-like series of films under the moniker of *Halloween*. They wanted to do a Halloween-related film each year with entirely different storylines, writers, and directors. If it had worked out, it would have been wonderful. Michael Myers fans and producers, however, didn't give it much of a chance, and we saw him return in Part Four. Of course now many people try to disown the part 4-6 timeline as well.

All in all, *Halloween* will always be one of the best horror movie franchises. It has inspired so many other films, and given us dozens of great cast members who have gone on to do so many amazing things. It is one of the few franchises which will probably still be being examined twenty years from now by a whole new generation of horror fans. Whether you like two, four, or all ten films, chances are you will be a lifelong fan and help to introduce it to new fans.

It is my hope that in writing this book, I too can inspire horror fans new and old to examine the films a little bit deeper and hopefully have some fun learning some things they didn't know.

WHAT'S IN A NAME?

As you might notice, a great deal of the category names are song titles or are music related. Music has always been a big part of my life, and many things revolve around it or can be related to it throughout my life. As such, it becomes very easy to find what might be the perfect category title within music that I like. The majority of the song titles used I actually do like. Some, of course, just fit too well for me not to use them. You will also notice I have a wide range of musical likes. I did the same thing in my *Friday the 13th* book, just not as extensively.

A prime example of both is the very first category, "I'm Your Boogeyman." How can I not use that song title, especially when it is remade by White Zombie? Or "I Want Out" by Helloween as the title of the category that covers how Michael escaped from different places throughout the films? Another great fit is "Trick or Treat" by Fastway, which is not only perfect for the subject matter but is also a song I really like, and pulls in another great horror film I love. (Think 1986, Skippy Handelman from *Family Ties*, Gene Simmons, and Ozzy Osbourne...not 2007's *Trick 'r Treat* which I also like, but not nearly as much.)

Of course, there is the occasional song or band I had never heard of like Wednesday 13's "Put Your Death Mask On." I listened to it and the song is decent, so

I couldn't pass it up for the Masks category.

I tried to use some song titles from people that actually appeared in the films. Luckily some good ones fit in well from LL Cool J, Weird Al Yankovic, and Rob Zombie, but I didn't manage to get someone like Busta Rhymes in the book.

My reasons for using some of the song titles will be very obvious: "Screaming in the Night" for Jamie Lee Curtis's category as she was the first Scream Queen of the franchise and "Whisper to a Scream" for the Danielle Harris category, since she didn't speak for the better part of Part 5.

Others, however, might not be so obvious, like "(O, What A) Lucky Man" by Emerson, Lake & Palmer for the Malcolm McDowell category. Once you learn that he made a semi-autobiographical film in 1973 titled *O, Lucky Man!*, though, it makes perfect sense.

Then there is the song "Laurie (Strange Things Happen)" by Dickey Lee – which I am sure very few have heard of – that fits in perfectly for obvious reasons. I almost didn't use it because I had never heard of it and figured no one else would have either. When my "research assistant" and friend, Brooksanne, presented it to me with the story that goes along with the song, I loved the idea of using it!

The song was written by a psychologist named Dr. Milton "Mitt" Addington. It was inspired by a story in a 1964 Memphis newspaper written by 15-year old Cathie Harmon, with whom he shared the royalties for the song. Harmon's story is believed to be inspired by the legend of Resurrection Mary. A series of young men claimed they encountered a shy young woman with very cold hands at dance parties in the Chicago area beginning as early as the 1930s. She would get a ride home from them but would ask to be dropped off at the Resurrection Cemetery. She would ask that the men not follow her as she walked home, and then she would simply vanish.

The story continues that a man named Jerry Palus met her at the Liberty Grove dance hall. This time, however, she gave him her actual home address. He would go to her house the following day and meet an older woman who told him that she did indeed have a daughter by that name, but that she had passed many years before. The photo she shared with him was the girl he had met the night before and dropped off at the cemetery.

So, keep in mind as you read through the book that some category names might mean something, while others might not. For a full list of the song titles and artists, please see the list at the back of the book. If it isn't in that list, then it was an unintentional use of a song title.

AN INTERVIEW WITH VICTOR MILLER

Since writing my first book, *6-13 A Friday the 13th Movie Trivia Book*, I have been lucky enough to build a relationship with the writer and creator of the original film that launched the entire franchise, Victor Miller. Victor is truly a horror icon, but beyond that he has won multiple awards and has been working/writing regularly ever since – including a new film which is in pre-production (*Rock Paper Dead*) that he co-wrote with Kerry Fleming, as well as a few other projects he is currently working on.

Victor was gracious enough to allow me to ask him a few questions about how his creation, *Friday the 13th*, has its roots in *Halloween* and more.

By now I am sure most have heard the story about Sean Cunningham calling you and saying how *Halloween* was doing so well and that you guys needed to copy it and make your own horror film. But recently, I heard you do an interview with Travis and Vic's Drunken Horror Adventures Podcast where you actually elaborated on how you learned how to write a successful horror film. Could you go into that story a bit?

My Yale English major and my Masters in Theatre at Tulane had taught me how to look at a piece of fiction and analyze how it worked or didn't. So, when I saw *Halloween* I figured out what Debra Hill and John Carpenter had done so well. Their roadmap was clean and clear: You need a few things: A prior evil which in some way poisons the universe of your film. Second you need a group of teenagers who are pretty, attractive and lively. Third you need a reason that the kids cannot be saved by the adult world around them. And then you need to pick off the "sinners" in really scary ways with a demonic figure whose motives are really credible---in other words, he/she cannot simply kill for the fun of it.

I have read that your favorite film is *Psycho*. John Carpenter liked it as well and went as far as naming a main character for a character from the film, Sam Loomis, as well as making Dr. Sam Loomis's nurse assistant named Marion.

How much did you draw from it or pay homage to it in the writing *Friday the 13ᵗʰ*, if at all? As a viewer/fan I see at least one, but wonder if it was intentional or just happened by coincidence. Annie, who we all think is a main character at the start of the film is soon killed off, similar to Marion in *Psycho*. I have even seen Robbie Morgan liken herself to Janet Leigh because of that.

Actually my favorite film is RAISING ARIZONA, but…Yes. In fact Sean called me early on and said we need an early kill, just like in PSYCHO because Hitchcock had demonstrated that you need to show that your killer is really REALLY serious enough to kill off a contract player. It won't work as well if you just slash up some "nobody" in your first ten minutes. You have to make your audience sit up and take notice. "Jesus, these guys are nuts!"

The second "homage" (which is code for copying which all good writers do) is in Jason popping out of the water in Alice's nightmare from her traumatic fight with Mrs. Voorhees. The dream-Jason out of the water and flash cut to the hospital bed is just about identical to the last scene in CARRIE.

If given the chance, would you have changed anything in the way that the end product of *Friday the 13ᵗʰ* was presented on screen, as we all know that writers don't always have control over what is presented to viewers in the end?

In filmmaker Eleanor Perry's BLUE PAGES she quotes something she overheard in a bar in Hollywood which goes something like this: "In Hollywood the writer is the woman." Once you choose to be a writer in film you know that you have just committed to a group craft which will involve the talents as well as the foibles of innumerable in-putters. But I would be an idiot to complain after 35 years of fame for my part in this amazing story, wouldn't I?

Is your new film, *Rock Paper Dead,* which has a cast full of horror icons, similar to *Friday the 13ᵗʰ* or *Halloween* in some ways? For instance, is there perhaps a kill scene that you said, "that worked so well in *F13* we need to put it in there," or does it follow the usual slasher film scenario that fans have come to love over the decades?

I would hope that I have improved in some of my skills over the past 3 and a half decades, but the main thrust of the film is that horrible people are created by circumstances and other horrendous acts. They don't just rise up from the lower depths of

Hell by accident. The Devil doesn't create horror, people do. And they do it to each other. I think that co-author Kerry Fleming and I have nailed it.

Best wishes with your book. If it had not been for Halloween the "holiday" or the movie, I might still be teaching teachers how to teach theatre. "Two roads diverged in a yellow road/ and sorry I could not travel both."

QUESTIONS

I met him, fifteen years ago; I was told there was nothing left; no reason, no conscience, no understanding; and even the most rudimentary sense of life or death, of good or evil, right or wrong. I met this six-year-old child, with this blank, pale, emotionless face, and the blackest eyes... the devil's eyes. I spent eight years trying to reach him, and then another seven trying to keep him locked up because I realized that what was living behind that boy's eyes was purely and simply... evil.

− Dr. Samuel Loomis

FAN QUESTIONS

When I began writing my *Friday the 13th* book, *6-13 A Friday the 13th Movie Trivia Book*, I attempted to get some horror fans to submit trivia questions to be in the book. Since no one knew me, I didn't get much of a response; there were four or five, but that was it.

I still really liked the idea of being able to include fans in my books, though, and tried again with this book. The response was much better, and the quality of questions submitted from the start was great. This led me to decide to use three questions from each person that submitted them. Of course this now means they each get their own page in the book, which makes me even more excited to share them and their questions with everyone.

You will see these questions are not categorized in any way. I did have to edit other categories to remove a question if it was submitted by a fan, so you won't find them in their expected categories.

I would like to thank Jessica, Ron, Clint, John, Luke, Tony, James, and Kevin for joining in and helping me make this book even better! I'm very happy to include such big *Halloween* fans in my book. I also shared a bit of information about each of them as they are all pretty exciting people, doing many diverse things in the horror community and elsewhere.

JESSICA FEENEY

Answers on page 253

Jessica Feeney, *aka* Little Miss Horror Nerd, is the co-host of "The Resurrection of Zombie 7" podcast. (See details and link in the final pages of this book.)

1) Which prolific voiceover actor was used to read Dr. Loomis's prologue, which is read over the opening credits of *Halloween H20: 20 Years Later*, rather than find and use the original audio done by Donald Pleasence for the original *Halloween* (1978)?
   a. Gary Owens
   b. Tom Kane
   c. Don Messick
   d. Frank Welker

2) Why did Danielle Harris not come back as Jamie Lloyd for *Halloween: The Curse of Michael Myers*?
   a. Scheduling conflict
   b. A dispute with the director
   c. Contract dispute and fate of her character
   d. She was recovering from an illness

3) What was Annie doing when she was attacked by Michael Myers in the 2007 *Halloween* remake?
   a. Having sex
   b. Trick-or-treating
   c. Carving a pumpkin
   d. Going to the bathroom

RON MARTIN
Answers on page 253

Ron Martin is the other co-host of "The Resurrection of Zombie 7" podcast.

1) What is the name of the company that produces the internet reality show in *Halloween: Resurrection?*
   a. Rhymes Entertainment
   b. Haddonfield Horror
   c. Dangertainment
   d. Horrortainment

2) What was the first gaming system to host a video game based on the *Halloween* movie franchise?
   a. Intellivision
   b. Atari 2600
   c. Colecovision
   d. Sega Genesis

3) Which original *Halloween* (1978) cast member has an uncredited voice cameo in *Halloween III: Season of the Witch?*
   a. Jamie Lee Curtis
   b. Donald Pleasence
   c. P.J. Soles
   d. Nick Castle

CLINT NARRAMORE
Answers on page 254

Clint Narramore is a huge horror fan who recently relocated from Minnesota to the Oklahoma Panhandle to become Program Director at country music radio station KGYN out of Guymon, Oklahoma.

1) The mask used in the original *Halloween* (1978) was of what famous TV character?
   a. Arthur Fonzarelli   c. James T. Kirk
   b. Frank Poncherello   d. Merrill Stubing

2) The characters of Dr. Samuel Loomis and his nurse assistant are named for characters from what iconic film?
   a. *Psycho*
   b. *Casablanca*
   c. *One Flew Over the Cuckoo's Nest*
   d. *Night of the Living Dead*

3) Which National Football League (NFL) team plays the *Halloween* theme at their home stadium when their opponent is faced with a 3rd down and long yardage situation?
   a. Minnesota Vikings
   b. Chicago Bears
   c. New Orleans Saints
   d. Cleveland Browns

JOHN CATHELINE
Answers on page 254

John Catheline is a professional wrestler working the independent circuit under his ring name, The Bouncer. His main promotion is Real Action Pro Wrestling (RAPW.net). He can currently be seen wrestling in the Ohio/Pennsylvania area.

1) In what row and plot number was Judith Myers buried?
   a. Row 13, Plot 31
   b. Row 18, Plot 20
   c. Row 31, Plot 66
   d. Row 10, Plot 31

2) What are the fictitious names of Tommy's three comic books that Laurie reads off in the original *Halloween* (1978)?
   a. *Spider-Man, Batman, The X-Men*
   b. *Black Vulcan, Apache Chief, Aquaman*
   c. *Laser Man, Neutron Man, Tarantula Man*
   d. *The Incredible Hulk, Guardians of the Galaxy, Superman*

3) In which three *Halloween* films does Dr. Wynn, the leader of the Cult of Thorn, appear?
   a. Parts 1, 5, and 6
   b. Parts 1, 2, and 6
   c. Parts 4, 5, and 6
   d. Parts 4, 5, and 8

LUKE SMALUK

Answers on page 255

Luke Smaluk is an avid horror fan. He has loved *Halloween* from a young age and is passing his love down to the next generation by introducing his six-year-old daughter to the horror classics as well as conventions. He is sure to teach her how to distinguish between what is real and what is cinema. Luke is also working on a horror screenplay that is loosely based on the origins of Halloween (the holiday).

1) Who provided the voice of Annie's boyfriend Paul in the original *Halloween* (1978)?
   a. Tommy Lee Wallace
   b. John Carpenter
   c. Rick Rosenthal
   d. Christopher Reeve

2) Which cast member suffered lacerations while filming a scene in *Halloween 4: The Return of Michael Myers*?
   a. Danielle Harris   c. Sasha Jenson
   b. Kathleen Kinmont   d. Ellie Cornell

3) Which two actors have portrayed Michael Myers more than once?
   a. Tyler Mane and George P. Wilbur
   b. Tyler Mane and Dick Warlock
   c. Tyler Mane and Brad Loree
   d. Tyler Mane and Don Shanks

TONY PROFFER
Answers on page 255

Tony Proffer is a film composer who has worked on independent films like *HI-8, Ghoulish Tales, Shark Exorcist,* and *Bite School.*

1) What song can be heard playing in Annie's car as she and Laurie are driving and being followed by Michael Myers in the original *Halloween* (1978)?
   a. "Mr. Sandman"
   b. "Christine Sixteen"
   c. "Don't Fear the Reaper"
   d. "Dream On"

2) What were the two main synthesizers that John Carpenter used to score the first three *Halloween* films, as well as his other early films?
   a. Sequential Circuits Prophet-5 and Prophet-10
   b. Roland Jupiter-4 and Jupiter-8
   c. Korg Trinity and Wavestation
   d. Yamaha DX-1 and DX-7

3) What relatively unusual time signature did John Carpenter use for the main music theme of *Halloween?*
   a. 9/8 time signature
   b. 5/4 time signature
   c. 2/2 time signature
   d. 3/8 time signature

JAMES MAXWELL
Answers on page 255

James Maxwell has been one of my biggest supporters right from the start. (He bought the second copy of the *Friday the 13th* book.) He now makes and sells complete *Friday the 13th* costumes and is starring in a fan film, *Deathcurse: Jason Returns.*

1) What can be seen on Michael Myers's hand when he smashes the window of Dr. Loomis and Nurse Marion Chambers's car while escaping from Smith's Grove in *Halloween* (1978)?
   a. Glove   c. Tattoo
   b. Scar   d. Wrench

2) Danny Strode has an action figure of which color Power Ranger on his nightstand in *Halloween: The Curse of Michael Myers*?
   a. Black   c. Yellow
   b. Red   d. Pink

3) What is the address of the house in which the Strode family is living in *Halloween: The Curse of Michael Myers*?
   a. 45 Lampkin Lane
   b. 666 Meridian Avenue
   c. 127 Carr Avenue
   d. 1428 Genesee Avenue

KEVIN S. KING
Answers on page 255

Kevin S. King is an avid horror collector and, some might say, a *Halloween* fanatic. He has begun creating and selling his own prop replicas as well. (See the last pages of this book for details on his Facebook group for collectors.)

1) What was the original working title for the film *Halloween?*
   a. *Trick-or-Treat*   c. *The Halloween Murders*
   b. *Psycho Killer*   d. *The Babysitter Murders*

2) Not counting John Carpenter, who is rumored to have worn the mask, how many different people portrayed Michael Myers/The Shape in the original *Halloween* (1978)?
   a. 3   c. 2
   b. 7   d. 5

3) What items did Sheriff Brackett say had been stolen from the hardware store in the original *Halloween* (1978)?
   a. An axe, a hammer, and some nails
   b. A drill, a sledgehammer, and rope
   c. A Halloween mask, rope, and a couple of knives
   d. A lock, some chain, and a knife

KEVIN'S CHRONOLOGY
Answers on page 256

Kevin suggested putting the kills of the first film in chronological order. I liked the idea, but made it a whole category of its own, and added on *Halloween II* as well. Put these Michael Myers kills in order from first to last.

Halloween (1978):
First - Sixth
   a. Lester the dog
   b. Bob Simms
   c. Judith Myers
   d. Lynda Van Der Klok
   e. Unnamed truck driver
   f. Annie Brackett

Halloween II (1981): (Note: Not all were killed by Michael Myers)
First – Tenth
   a. Budd Scarlotti
   b. Jill Franco
   c. Marshall
   d. Mr. Garrett
   e. Dr. Frederick Mixter
   f. Ben Tramer
   g. Nurse Virginia Alves
   h. Alice Martin
   i. Janet Newhall
   j. Karen Rainey

Kevin also shared a theory with me, one that I totally believe to be true and, as far as either of us have seen or heard, has not been specifically shared before. Kevin gets total credit for this; I just agree with him.

The pumpkin that Laurie (Jamie Lee Curtis) carves up in the Doyles' kitchen is later carved up a bit more and repurposed to shoot the opening sequence to the film.

If you examine the photos on the following page, particularly the circled areas, you will see the matching markings. It is hard to believe that any two pumpkins could be so similar. When you add in the fact that the film had such a low budget that actors brought some of their own wardrobes, and that they gathered up paper leaves after scenes so they could be used again, it is not that much of a stretch to think they reused a pumpkin.

On the top is the pumpkin used in the iconic opening sequence of the film, and below it is Laurie carrying her carved pumpkin out of the kitchen in the film.

While I know there is no real trivia question here, I strive to bring you unique and trivial facts like this in my books. A big thanks to Kevin for bringing this to my (our) attention.

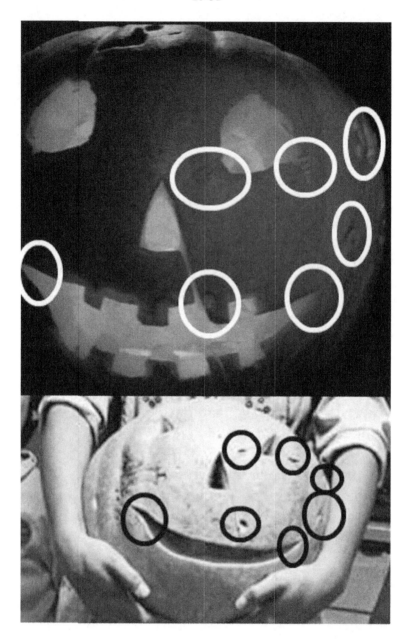

"Death has come to your little town, sheriff."
– Dr. Samuel Loomis (Halloween (1978))

I'M YOUR BOOGEYMAN

Answers on page 257

Questions all about Michael Myers.

1) What was Michael Myers's mother's name in the 2007 remake?

2) How old was Michael Myers when he killed his sister Judith in the original *Halloween* (1978)?

3) How old was Michael Myers when he killed his sister Judith in the *Halloween* (2007) remake?

4) In *Halloween: The Curse of Michael Myers*, Tommy Doyle explains that Michael has been affected by what curse?

5) What does Michael Myers write in blood on the blackboard at the elementary school he breaks into in *Halloween II* (1981)?

6) What costume was Michael Myers wearing while killing his sister Judith in the original *Halloween* (1978)?

7) According to the original timeline, when was Michael Myers born?
   a. October 31, 1956
   b. June 13, 1957
   c. October 19, 1957
   d. October 13, 1956

8) According to additional scenes in the television version of the original *Halloween* (1978), what was Michael Myers's middle name?
   a. Aaron
   b. Alexander
   c. Austin
   d. Audrey

9) The name "The Shape," given to Michael Myers whenever he is wearing the mask, was taken from a term used during what historical event?
   a. Spanish Inquisition
   b. Charles Manson's trial
   c. Salem Witch Trials
   d. Ed Gein's trial

10) What is the only word we ever hear adult Michael Myers say in any of the ten *Halloween* films?
   a. "Die"
   b. "Mom"
   c. "Boo"
   d. "Kill"

11) Who is the first person we see Michael kill while wearing the traditional Michael Myers mask in the 2007 *Halloween* remake?
   a. Ronnie White
   b. Judith Myers
   c. Lynda Van Der Klok
   d. Ismael Cruz

12) What does Michael Myers use to kill his first human victim in the 2007 *Halloween* remake?
   a. Butcher knife
   b. Axe
   c. Tree branch
   d. Bare hands

13) Who does Michael Myers take his blue coveralls from in the 2007 *Halloween* remake?
   a. Bubba Brownlee
   b. Rollo
   c. Big Joe Grizzly
   d. Big Benny

PARENTS JUST DON'T UNDERSTAND
Answers on page 258

Questions all about Michael Myers's parents.

1) Where does Deborah Myers work in the 2007 *Halloween* remake?
   a. The Red Cat
   b. The Rabbit in Red
   c. The Blue Rabbit
   d. The Black Dog

2) What was the name of Michael Myers's father in the original *Halloween* (1978)?
   a. Charles
   b. Peter
   c. Ronnie
   d. Michael

3) Although not mentioned or credited in the original *Halloween* (1978), Michael Myers's mother was given what name in a 1979 novelization of the film?
   a. Edith
   b. Maureen
   c. Alice
   d. Deborah

4) In the original storyline, how did Michael Myers's parents die?
   a. Murder-suicide
   b. Car crash
   c. Plane crash
   d. Train crash

5) In the remake storyline, how does Deborah Myers kill herself?
   a. Gunshot
   b. Carbon monoxide poisoning
   c. Crashes car into a tree
   d. Hanging

BACK HOME AGAIN
Answers on page 258

Questions all about Haddonfield, Illinois.

1) According to the "Entering Haddonfield" sign in *Halloween II* (2009), in what year did Haddonfield become an incorporated city?
   a. 1692   c. 1883
   b. 1784   d. 1931

2) The Haddonfield sign says that it is the "Home of the" what?
   a. Huskies   c. Hippos
   b. Bears   d. Mustangs

3) In what year was Halloween banned in Haddonfield, according to *Halloween: The Curse of Michael Myers*?
   a. 1978   c. 1989
   b. 1984   d. 1992

4) In which county is Haddonfield, Illinois located?
   a. Wessex County   c. Carpenter County
   b. Stanley County   d. Livingston County

#SLASHTAGS

Answers on page 258

Match these taglines with their movies:

1. It's gonna be one hell of a family reunion!

2. Blood is thicker than water

3. Evil has a destiny

4. He came back to finish what they'll never forget …

5. The night he came home

6. Michael lives, and this time they're ready!

7. Evil finds its way home

8. The night no one comes home

9. Family is forever

10. Everyone knows his name. Now, everyone will know the truth.

#SLASHTAGS

a. *Halloween (1978)*

b. *Halloween II (1981)*

c. *Halloween III: Season of the Witch*

d. *Halloween 4: The Return of Michael Myers*

e. *Halloween 5: The Revenge of Michael Myers*

f. *Halloween: The Curse of Michael Myers*

g. *Halloween H20: 20 Years Later*

h. *Halloween: Resurrection*

i. *Halloween (2007)*

j. *Halloween II (2009)*

SOME FOLKS

Answers on page 259

Questions all about some random people within the *Halloween* franchise.

1) Who owned the bar and got the mob/posse together after he tried calling the police station and didn't get an answer in *Halloween 4: The Return of Michael Myers?*

2) What is the name of the guidance counselor at Hillcrest Academy High School in *Halloween H20: 20 Years Later?*

3) Who creates the Dangertainment show in *Halloween: Resurrection?*

4) What is the name of the janitor who works his way up to being a guard at Smith's Grove Sanitarium in the 2007 *Halloween* remake?

5) What is the name of the wealthy Irishman that created the Silver Shamrock Novelties toy factory in *Halloween III: Season of the Witch?*

6) Who is in charge of the control room for the Dangertainment show in *Halloween: Resurrection?*

7) What was the name of the power worker that Michael Myers throws into the transformers in *Halloween 4: The Return of Michael Myers?*
   a. Carlton   c. Bucky
   b. Jeff   d. Greg

8) What are the names of the mother and her daughter that Michael steals a car from at a rest area on Highway 139 in *Halloween H20: 20 Years Later?*
   a. Claudia and Casey   c. Lisa and Rachel
   b. Sara and Andy   d. Mary and Fran

9) What was the name of the girl that drove Rachel to pick up Jamie from school in *Halloween 4: The Return of Michael Myers?*
   a. Angela   c. Amber
   b. Kelly   d. Lindsey

10) What is the name of the principal at Michael Myers's school in the 2007 *Halloween* remake?
   a. Principal Smithers
   b. Principal Chambers
   c. Principal Anderson
   d. Principal Kirk

11) What is the name of the man that is killed in the hospital at the start of *Halloween III: Season of the Witch?*
   a. Harry Grimbridge   c. Brian Grand
   b. Raymond Graham   d. Frederick Garrison

12) What is the name of the sanitarium patient that is a serial killer buff in *Halloween: Resurrection*?
   a. Patrick
   b. Larry
   c. Harold
   d. Roy

13) Who is the caretaker at the cemetery where Deborah Myers was buried in the 2007 *Halloween* remake?
   a. Chester Chesterfield
   b. Andrew Andrews
   c. Frank Franklin
   d. Rob Roberts

14) What is the name of Dr. Daniel Challis's wife in *Halloween III: Season of the Witch*?
   a. Vanessa
   b. Veronica
   c. Linda
   d. Eva

15) Who owns The Rabbit in Red where Deborah Myers used to work in *Halloween II* (2009)?
   a. Big Joe Grizzly
   b. Big Lou Martini
   c. Tiny Max Brown
   d. Bob Smith

16) What is the name of the little boy dressed as a clown that asks Michael if he is a giant and if they can be friends in *Halloween II* (2009)?
   a. Michael
   b. Paul
   c. Cooper
   d. Mark

17) What is the name of the businessman from San Diego that is in Santa Mira to visit the Silver Shamrock Novelties factory in *Halloween III: Season of the Witch*?
   a. Ron Harper
   b. John Kemper
   c. Buddy Kupfer
   d. Roger Stevensen

18) What is the name of the emcee for Phantom Jam in *Halloween II* (2009)?
   a. Uncle Seymour Coffins
   b. Big Daddy Cool
   c. Brother Love Jackson
   d. Terrible Terry

19) What was the name of the boy Rachel had to break a date with so she could babysit Jamie in *Halloween 4: The Return of Michael Myers*?
   a. Danny
   b. Brady
   c. Zach
   d. Mikey

PSYCHO KILLER

Answers on page 260

Which Michael Myers actor...

1) portrayed a character named Thorn in *Black Masks 2: City of Masks*, alongside the likes of *Saw* star Tobin Bell and professional wrestler Rob Van Dam?

2) portrayed Lieutenant Saunders in *The Running Man*, and has done stunts on films like *Silence of the Lambs*, *Blacula*, *Re-Animator*, and *A Nightmare on Elm Street 5: The Dream Child*?

3) is actually from a town named Haddonfield in New Jersey?

4) has portrayed a Klingon, a Cardassian, and a Jem'Hadar, and was Leonard Nimoy's stunt double for *Star Trek: The Motion Picture*?

5) directed the 1990 TV mini-series version of Stephen King's *It*?

6) has said in interviews that he thought he was trying out for a part as actor Mike Myers's stunt double, and found out at the audition that he was going to be the movie killer instead?

7) portrayed the guard in the memorable Vulcan Pinch scene of the film *Spaceballs*?

8) portrayed the recurring character Nakoma on the TV series *The Life and Times of Grizzly Adams?*

9) actually wrote a pirate-vs.-vampire script titled *Duel* when he was just eight years old, which he directed and edited when he was nine?

10) worked on John Carpenter's *The Fog* and *Escape From New York* as well as classic disaster films like *The Poseidon Adventure, Earthquake,* and *The Towering Inferno?*

11) was one of five stunt performers to appear as the killer in the costume in *Scream 2,* which is shown on a TV in *Halloween H20: Twenty Years Later?*

12) has directed films like *Dennis the Menace* (1993), *The Last Starfighter,* and *Major Payne?*

13) did stunt work on the TV shows *Twin Peaks* and *Northern Exposure?*

a. Debra Hill	h. Daeg Faerch
b. Nick Castle	i. Tyler Mane
c. Dick Warlock	j. James Winburn
d. Tom Morga	k. Tommy Lee Wallace
e. Don Shanks	l. George P. Wilbur
f. Chris Durand	m. A. Michael Lerner
g. Brad Loree	

"Michael Myers is a killer shark in baggy-ass overalls who gets his kicks from killing everyone and everything he comes across."
— Freddie Harris (Halloween: Resurrection)

THE REAL ME
Answers on page 260

More questions about the actors that have portrayed Michael Myers.

1) Which Michael Myers actor was once a professional wrestler under the name Big Sky and was a frequent tag team partner of Vinnie Vegas, *aka* Kevin Nash/Diesel?

2) Which Michael Myers actor has also portrayed Jason Voorhees and Leatherface?

3) Tony Moran is actually the older brother of which actress?

4) Daeg Faerch went on to portray a character named Michel in which film?

5) Which character did Tyler Mane portray in the original *X-Men* movie in 2000?
   a. Beast
   b. Pyro
   c. Sabretooth
   d. Young Magneto

6) Adam Gunn, who was Young Michael Myers in *Halloween II* (1981), once did commercials for which breakfast cereal?
   a. Golden Grahams
   b. Honeycomb
   c. Trix
   d. Cookie Crisp

7) In what film from Tyler Mane's Mane Entertainment does he star alongside fellow *Halloween* cast members Leslie Easterbrook, Ranae Geerlings, and Daniel Roebuck, as well as *Friday the 13th* alumni Derek Mears and Todd Farmer?
   a. *The Horror Show*
   b. *Compound Fracture*
   c. *Chopper*
   d. *Penance Lane*

"The child christened Michael Myers has become a sort of ghost, a mere shape of a human being, and there's nothing left here now."
— Dr. Loomis (Halloween (2007))

BEND ME, SHAPE ME

A comprehensive list of everyone to ever portray Michael Myers.

Halloween (1978)	
Actor	**Notes**
Debra Hill	Michael in the opening scenes while Judith is being killed. The only female to portray Michael.
Will Sandin	Michael Age 6. Sandin had an additional scene in the TV version of the film. That scene was filmed during the production of *Halloween II* (1981) and he had clearly gone through a growth spurt in the time between shooting his scenes.
Nick Castle	Earned just $25 a day.
Tony Moran	Michael Myers unmasked. Listed at 23 years old in the credits, but Michael was 21.
Tommy Lee Wallace	Wallace was doing Production Design and Editing for the film.
Jim Winburn	Additional Stunt Man
John Carpenter	It has been said that Carpenter wore the mask in one scene, but no one knows which scene it is.
Halloween II (1981)	
Adam Gunn	Young Michael Myers
Dick Warlock	Was also Patrol Man #3

Halloween 4: The Return of Michael Myers	
George P. Wilbur	One of only two people to portray Michael Myers in multiple films. (See Part 6 and Tyler Mane)
Erik Preston	Additional Stunt Man
Tom Morga	Only person to portray Michael Myers, Jason Voorhees, and Leatherface.

Halloween 5: The Revenge of Michael Myers	
Don Shanks	

Halloween: The Curse of Michael Myers	
George P. Wilbur	
A. Michael Lerner	Additional Stunt Man

Halloween H20: Twenty Years Later	
Chris Durand	

Halloween: Resurrection	
Brad Loree	
Gary J. Clayton	Young Michael Myers in an alternate opening sequence.

Halloween (2007)	
Tyler Mane	The tallest actor to portray Michael Myers.
Daeg Faerch	Young Michael Myers

Halloween II (2009)	
Tyler Mane	Just the second person to portray Michael Myers in two films.
Chase Wright Vanek	Young Michael Myers

"Was that the Boogeyman?"
– Laurie Strode (Halloween (1978/2007))

LAURIE (STRANGE THINGS HAPPEN)

Answers on page 261

Questions all about Laurie Strode.

1) What was Laurie Strode's real name at birth in
   Halloween II (2009)?

2) What was Laurie Strode's new name after she
   faked her death?

3) Laurie Strode has a "tramp stamp" tattoo of what
   in *Halloween II* (2009)?
   a. Butterfly   c. Hockey mask
   b. Dog   d. Skull

4) What did Laurie use to stab Michael Myers in the
   neck in the original *Halloween* (1978)?
   a. Butcher knife   c. Scissors
   b. Pen   d. Knitting needle

5) What are the names of Laurie Strode's parents in
   the 2007 *Halloween* remake?
   a. John and Debra   c. Mason and Cynthia
   b. Michael and Fran   d. Howard and Marion

6) Laurie tells Tommy and Lindsey to go to what family's house to call for help in the original *Halloween* (1978)?
   a. The McKenzies
   b. The Webbs
   c. The Bracketts
   d. The Tramers

7) Laurie Strode has a nightmare about killing which person in *Halloween II* (2009)?
   a. Sheriff Brackett
   b. Annie Brackett
   c. Michael Myers
   d. Dr. Loomis

8) Where does Laurie Strode work in *Halloween II* (2009)?
   a. The Old Town Reader Book Store
   b. The Rabbit in Red Lounge
   c. Uncle Meat's Java Hole
   d. Vincent Drug Store

9) What does Laurie Strode do to Michael Myers right before letting go and falling to her death in *Halloween: Resurrection*?
   a. Kisses him
   b. Hugs him
   c. Gives him the finger
   d. Bites him

10) What is Keri Tate's (Laurie Strode's) job title in
Halloween H20: 20 Years Later?
a. Principal
b. Dean of Students
c. Vice Principal
d. Headmistress

11) What does Laurie Strode say the inkblot on her
therapist's wall looks like to her?
a. Butterfly
b. Elephant
c. White horse
d. Dragon

12) Which textbook did Laurie forget at school in the
original *Halloween* (1978)?
a. Algebra
b. Chemistry
c. U.S. History
d. French

THE WHICH DOCTOR?

Answers on page 261

Match the doctor to the proper fact.

Which doctor:

1) treated Laurie Strode in the hospital after the events of the original 1978 film took place?

2) led a group of costumed druids in a search for Jamie Lloyd's baby?

3) ran Smith's Grove Sanitarium in the remake?

4) was Laurie Strode's therapist?

5) was in charge of the Haddonfield Children's Clinic?

6) informed Dr. Loomis and Dr. Wynn that Jamie Lloyd had very recently given birth before her death?

7) attempted to thwart a plot to kill millions of children on Halloween?

8) was the Medical Administrator that transferred Michael Myers back to Smith's Grove Sanitarium from Ridgemont Federal Sanitarium?

a. Dr. Bonham
b. Dr. Max Hart
c. Dr. Wynn
d. Dr. Barbara Collier

e. Dr. Mixter
f. Dr. Daniel Challis
g. Dr. Hoffman
h. Dr. Koplensen

"Inside every one of us there exists a dark side. Most people rise above it, but some are consumed by it. Until there is nothing left but pure evil."
– Dr. Samuel Loomis (Halloween (2009))

THE DEVIL AND I
Answers on page 262

Questions all about Dr. Samuel Loomis.

1) How many times did Dr. Loomis shoot Michael Myers during the altercation in the Doyle household, which sent Michael over the balcony railing in *Halloween* (1978)?

2) The father of which of Michael Myers's victims shows up at Dr. Loomis's book signing with a gun in *Halloween II* (2009)?

3) A police officer said he had heard about Dr. Loomis on what television news show in *Halloween H20: Twenty Years Later*?

4) How many of the *Halloween* films did Donald Pleasence appear in as Dr. Samuel Loomis?

5) What was the name of the first book written by Dr. Loomis about his time spent with young Michael Myers at the Smith's Grove Sanitarium in *Halloween* (2007)?

6) What type of gun does Dr. Loomis buy in the 2007 *Halloween* remake?
   a. .44 caliber revolver
   b. .38 Special revolver
   c. .357 Magnum
   d. 9MM pistol

7) During Dr. Loomis's book signing, a fan named Chett Johns asks Loomis to sign his book to whom in *Halloween II* (2009)?
   a. "Chett, Michael Myers's #1 Fan"
   b. "Chett, The Bringer of Death"
   c. "Your #1 Fan, Chett"
   d. "Chett Myers, The Other Son"

8) Dr. Loomis appears on what television talk show in *Halloween II* (2009)?
   a. *The Jerry Show*
   b. *Late Night Talk with George*
   c. *Kramer's Korner*
   d. *The Newman Hour*

9) What was the name of the Reverend that picks up Dr. Loomis in *Halloween 4: The Return of Michael Myers*?
   a. Reverend Jim Ignatowski
   b. Reverend Aaron Gilstrom
   c. Reverend Jackson P. Sayer
   d. Reverend Shepherd Book

10) What was the title of Dr. Loomis's second book about Michael Myers, in which he reveals Laurie Strode is indeed Michael's baby sister, Angel, in *Halloween II* (2009)?
   a. *The Devil's World*   c. *Pure Evil*
   b. *The Man Behind the*   d. *The Devil Walks Among*
      Mask   *Us*

11) According to Dr. Loomis in the *Halloween II* remake, what is the name of his aunt?
   a. Vera   c. Shelly
   b. Chris   d. Debbie

12) What is the name of the woman that Dr. Loomis was engaged to in one of the *Halloween* comics series?
   a. Debra Hill   c. Andrea Parker
   b. Luanne Platter   d. Jennifer Hill

13) In the comic *Halloween: One Good Scare*, Dr. Loomis is given a son who follows in his footsteps as a doctor at Smith's Grove Sanitarium; what was his son's name?
   a. Michael   c. Jason
   b. David   d. Frederick

14) Six years before *Halloween: The Curse of Michael Myers* takes place, Dr. Loomis suffered from which medical event?
   a. Stroke   c. Collapsed lung
   b. Heart attack   d. Broken back

"What scares me is what scares you. We're all afraid of the same things. That's why horror is such a powerful genre. All you have to do is ask yourself what frightens you and you'll know what frightens me."
— John Carpenter

THE MASTER OF HORROR
Answers on page 263

Questions all about John Carpenter.

1) Which John Carpenter film opens with the Edgar Allan Poe quote, "Is *all* that we see or seem/ But a dream within a dream?"

2) What was the first major studio film made by John Carpenter?

3) John Carpenter had a son named Cody with which actress that has been in multiple Carpenter films?

4) The screenplay for John Carpenter's *The Thing* was written by which famous actor's son?
a. Donald Sutherland   c. Leslie Nielsen
b. Michael Douglas   d. Burt Lancaster

5) In 2005-06, John Carpenter directed two episodes of which horror TV series – one featuring *The Walking Dead*'s Norman Reedus and the other Derek Mears from the *Friday the 13th* 2009 reboot?
a. *The Twilight Zone*   c. *Fringe*
b. *Supernatural*   d. *Masters of Horror*

6) What other *Friday the 13th* reboot cast member starred in John Carpenter's *The Ward*?
   a. Danielle Panabaker
   b. Amanda Righetti
   c. Willa Ford
   d. America Olivio

7) What was the name of the band that consisted of John Carpenter, Nick Castle, and Tommy Lee Wallace?
   a. The Coupe de Villes
   b. The Monte Carlos
   c. The Mustangs
   d. The Pintos

8) What John Carpenter film was based on the Ray Nelson short story titled *Eight O'clock in the Morning*?
   a. *In the Mouth of Madness*
   b. *Assault on Precinct 13*
   c. *They Live*
   d. *The Fog*

9) What John Carpenter film was based on the only novel written by author H.F. Saint?
   a. *Prince of Darkness*
   b. *Escape from New York*
   c. *Big Trouble in Little China*
   d. *Memoirs of an Invisible Man*

10) Who co-wrote the sci-fi comedy *Dark Star* with John Carpenter, and then went on to write the screenplays for *Alien, Total Recall,* and *The Return of the Living Dead?*
    a. Dan O'Bannon
    b. Nick Castle
    c. Bill Phillips
    d. Martin Quatermass

11) John Carpenter wrote the theme music to what 2015 NBC summer series, based on a story by James Patterson?
    a. *Rookie Blue*
    b. *Taxi Brooklyn*
    c. *Murder in the First*
    d. *Zoo*

12) John Carpenter's former wife, Adrienne Barbeau, provided the voice of the computer in which of Carpenter's films?
    a. *Escape From L.A.*
    b. *The Thing*
    c. *Dark Star*
    d. *Starman*

FINE CARPENTRY

A list of all the films directed or written by John Carpenter, which featured cast members from the *Halloween* film franchise.

Directed By:
Donald Pleasence (2)
Escape from New York
Prince of Darkness
Jamie Lee Curtis (2)
The Fog
Escape from New York
Nick Castle (2)
Dark Star
Escape from New York
James Winburn (1)
The Fog
Charles Cyphers (5)
Assault on Precinct 13
Someone's Watching Me (TV)
Elvis (TV)
The Fog
Escape from New York
Nancy Keyes (2)
Assault on Precinct 13
The Fog
Robert Phalen (2)
Someone's Watching Me (TV)
Starman
Tommy Lee Wallace (1)
The Fog
Tom Atkins (2)
The Fog
Escape from New York

Nancy Stephens (1)
Escape from New York
Carmen Filpi (1)
Escape from New York
Written By:
Donald Pleasence (1)
Better Late Than Never (TV)
Brad Dourif (1)
Eyes of Laura Mars
P.J. Soles (1)
Zuma Beach

Halloween: The Curse of Michael Myers jack-o-lantern

COME TOGETHER

Answers on page 264

Many of the *Halloween* franchise cast members have worked together on other projects. Here are some questions about those other films and TV shows.

1) Which *Halloween* movie director also directed the sequel to John Carpenter's film *Vampires?*

2) In what film directed by Nick Castle did Lance Guest (Jimmy, *Halloween II* (1981)) portray both Alex Rogan and Beta Alex?

3) Michael Currie (Rafferty, Part 3) portrayed Sheriff/Constable Carter alongside Mitchell Ryan (Dr. Wynn, Part 6) as Burke Devlin on what popular TV series set in Collinsport, Maine?

4) *Halloween* franchise alums Ellie Cornell, Charles Cyphers, Marianne Hagan, Brad Loree, and P.J. Soles all appeared in what 2006 film about a young couple that inherits a house, only to find they can communicate with the dead on their second floor phone?
   a. *976-EVIL*
   b. *Dead Calling*
   c. *1-900-DEAD-CEL*
   d. *Purgatory Calling*

5) Ken Foree (Big Joe Grizzly, Remake) and
   Kristina Klebe (Lynda, Remake) star as Interpol
   agents that must team with a dangerous prisoner
   to fight off zombies in what 2009 horror film?
   a. *Zone of the Dead*   c. *Island of the Zombies*
   b. *Zombieland*   d. *Zombie Pods From Space*

6) Marianne Hagan appeared alongside Danielle
   Harris in what 2010 vampire horror?
   a. *Cold Prey 3*   c. *My Soul To Take*
   b. *Stake Land*   d. *The Presence*

7) Leslie Easterbrook (Patty Frost, Remake)
   portrayed Debbie Callahan in all but one
   installment of what other long-running movie
   franchise, including Part 2, which featured
   Howard Hesseman (Uncle Meat, Remake 2) as
   well?
   a. *Lethal Weapon*   c. *Final Destination*
   b. *Die Hard*   d. *Police Academy*

8) Mitchell Ryan (Dr. Wynn, Part 6) portrayed
   which magazine publisher in *Death of a Centerfold:
   The Dorothy Stratten Story*, which starred Jamie Lee
   Curtis in the title role?
   a. Bob Guccione   c. Hugh Hefner
   b. Larry Flynt   d. Jerry Caesar

9) Tamara Glynn (Samantha, Part 5) portrayed Tammy the Paramedic in what film that also featured Jamie Lee Curtis and was written and directed by Billy Bob Thornton – who was also the star of the film?
   a. *Intolerable Cruelty*   c. *Sling Blade*
   b. *Daddy and Them*   d. *Mr. Woodcock*

10) Rick Rosenthal directed Malcolm McDowell in an episode of what TV show in 1998?
   a. *The Twilight Zone*
   b. *Tales from the Dark Side*
   c. *Fantasy Island*
   d. *Tales from the Crypt*

11) Tom Atkins (Dr. Challis, Part 3) portrayed heroin dealer Michael Hunsaker and Mitchell Ryan (Dr. Wynn, Part 6) played The General in which 1980s blockbuster film?
   a. *Tango & Cash*
   b. *Beverly Hills Cop*
   c. *The Falcon and the Snowman*
   d. *Lethal Weapon*

I WANT OUT

A list of the ways that Michael Myers has escaped from the custody of law enforcement and the sanitariums throughout the films.

FILM	ESCAPE METHOD
Halloween (1978)	Michael breaks through a window in his cell door and manages to get out. He then releases all the inmates at Smith's Grove. When Dr. Loomis and Marion show up to get him, he steals their car.
Halloween II (19981)	Didn't escape from anywhere as he was already on the loose.
Halloween 4: The Return of Michael Myers	Kills all the ambulance attendants while being transferred from a maximum security facility back to Smith's Grove.
Halloween 5: The Revenge of Michael Myers	Broken out of jail at the end by the mysterious man in black. Jamie Lloyd is also kidnapped at the same time.
Halloween: The Curse of Michael Myers	At the end of the Producer's Cut, he switches clothes with Dr. Wynn and walks out of Smith's Grove.
Halloween H20: Twenty Years Later	Michael switches clothes again at the end and gets away wearing a paramedic uniform.

Halloween: Resurrection	He didn't escape from anywhere as he was already on the loose. In the end, we see his eyes open while on the coroner's table, but do not see any escape.
Halloween (2007)	Michael escapes his cell after two orderlies ridicule him and abuse a female inmate. He then kills everyone working that night and escapes that morning.
Halloween II (2009)	The coroner's van carrying Michael's body hits a cow. Michael uses this opportunity to escape the van.

Opening sequence *Halloween II* (1981) jack-o-lantern

A SPOOKY LITTLE GIRL LIKE YOU
Answers on page 264

Questions all about Jamie Lloyd.

1) Which family takes in orphaned Jamie Lloyd in
   Halloween 4: The Return of Michael Myers?
   a. The Strodes   c. The Greens
   b. The Blankenships   d. The Carrutherses

2) What is the name of the yearly Halloween
   costume show held by the Haddonfield
   Children's Clinic?
   a. Goblin Costume Pageant
   b. Ghoul's Night Pageant
   c. The Ghost Party
   d. All Hallows Eve Party

3) What was Darlene Carruthers doing when Jamie
   Lloyd stabbed her with a pair of scissors?
   a. Sleeping
   b. Driving
   c. Running a bath
   d. Walking the dog

4) What did Jamie call Michael Myers as she was
   laying in the coffin, which got him to stop trying
   to kill her momentarily in *Halloween 5: The Revenge
   of Michael Myers?*
   a. Uncle Michael   c. Uncle Mikey
   b. Uncle M   d. Uncle Boogeyman

5) In the theatrical version of *Halloween 6: The Curse of Michael Myers*, Jamie Lloyd is killed by her uncle Michael using which piece of farming equipment?
   a. Corn thresher   c. Reaper
   b. Hay baler   d. Harrow

6) In the producer's cut of *Halloween 6: The Curse of Michael Myers*, who kills Jamie Lloyd (instead of her uncle Michael)?
   a. Tommy Doyle   c. Dr. Loomis
   b. Mrs. Blankenship   d. Dr. Terence Wynn

7) Which actress took over the role of Jamie Lloyd for *Halloween 6: The Curse of Michael Myers* after producers and Danielle Harris could not come to an agreement?
   a. Melissa Joan Hart   c. Katee Sackhoff
   b. J.C. Brandy   d. Danielle Panabaker

A *Halloween* Movie Trivia Book

"You don't really know much about Halloween. You thought no further than the strange custom of having your children wear masks and go out begging for candy."
– Conal Cochran (Halloween III: Season of the Witch)

TRICK OR TREAT
Answers on page 265

Questions all about some of the different costumes worn by characters in the films.

1) What was Tommy Doyle dressed as in the original *Halloween* (1978)?
   a. Dog   c. Astronaut
   b. Ghost   d. Soldier

2) Which character explained her Halloween costume as "a chick dressing up as a dude who wants to be a chick" in *Halloween II* (2009)?
   a. Wendy Snow   c. Laurie Strode
   b. Jane Salvador   d. Harley David

3) What does Jamie Lloyd dress up as for the Goblin Costume Pageant in *Halloween 5: The Revenge of Michael Myers*?
   a. Doctor   c. Clown
   b. Princess   d. Angel

4) What was the boy who was at the emergency room when Laurie arrived to the hospital dressed as in *Halloween II* (1981)?
   a. Frog   c. Pirate
   b. Wizard   d. Clown

5) Which of the Silver Shamrock Novelties Halloween masks is little Buddy Kupfer wearing when he is used as the example of what will happen when the whole country watches the giveaway at 9 PM in *Halloween III: Season of the Witch*?

6) Which mask is Dr. Daniel Challis forced to wear while tied to a chair to watch the Horrorthon and Silver Shamrock Giveaway in *Halloween III: Season of the Witch*?

7) What does Laurie Strode say was the last costume she wore for Halloween in the *Halloween* (2007) remake?
   a. Dead Little Red Riding Hood
   b. Zombie
   c. Jason Voorhees
   d. Gene Simmons

8) Myles and Scott dress as what duo in *Halloween: Resurrection*?
   a. Fred Flintstone and Barney Rubble
   b. Batman and Robin
   c. Jeff Spicoli and Mr. Hand
   d. Vincent Vega and Jules Winnfield

9) The three children who tease Jamie at school
about her uncle Michael were wearing what
costumes in *Halloween 4: The Return of Michael
Myers*?
   a. Spider-Man, Iron Man, Dyna Girl
   b. M.A.S.K.'s Matt Trakker, Frankenstein,
   Penguin
   c. Dracula, Ronald Reagan, She-Ra Princess of
   Power
   d. Yogi Bear, Scooby-Doo, Dick Dastardly

10) Laurie, Mya, and Harley dress up as characters
from what cult classic film to go to Phantom Jam
in *Halloween II* (2009)?
   a. *The Texas Chainsaw Massacre*
   b. *A Clockwork Orange*
   c. *The Rocky Horror Picture Show*
   d. *Monty Python and the Holy Grail*

"That is not appropriate babysitter behavior!"
– Tommy Doyle (Halloween (2007))

MONSTER MATCH-UP
Answers on page 265

Match the character to the costume they wore in a Halloween film.

1) Billy Hill
2) Laurie Strode (2007)
3) Bella Challis
4) Lindsey Wallace (2007)
5) Jamie Lloyd (*Halloween 4: The Return of Michael Myers*)
6) Tim Strode
7) Samantha Thomas
8) Beth
9) Big Lou Martini
10) Tina Williams
11) Willie Challis

    a. Silver Shamrock Skull
    b. Frankenstein
    c. Frankenstein
    d. Silver Shamrock Witch
    e. Slutty Vampire
    f. Slutty Devil
    g. Bride of Frankenstein
    h. Clown
    i. Pirate
    j. Queen of Sheba
    k. Magenta – a Domestic

SWEET LITTLE SISTER
Answers on page 266

Questions all about Judith Myers.

1) How old was Judith Myers when Michael killed her in the original *Halloween* (1978)?
   a. 13   c. 15
   b. 14   d. 17

2) How many times does Michael Myers stab his sister Judith in the original *Halloween* (1978)?
   a. 3 times   c. 10 times
   b. 8 times   d. 13 times

3) According to the reporter, how many times did Michael Myers stab his sister Judith in the 2007 *Halloween* remake?
   a. 8 times   c. 17 times
   b. 12 times   d. 31 times

4) What time of night was it when Michael Myers killed his sister Judith in the original *Halloween* (1978), as can be determined by the clock in the opening scenes of the film?
   a. A few minutes after 10:00P.M.
   b. A few minutes after 8:00P.M.
   c. 11:34P.M.
   d. 12:04A.M.

5) What was Judith Myers's middle name, as can be seen on her tombstone in the original *Halloween* (1978)?
   a. Audrey
   b. Pamela
   c. Margaret
   d. Laurie

6) In the original *Halloween* (1978), actor David Kyle was simply listed as Judith's Boyfriend, but in the 1979 novelization of the film he is named what?
   a. David
   b. Donald
   c. Steven
   d. Danny

7) What was the name of Judith Myers's boyfriend in the 2007 *Halloween* remake?
   a. Danny Hughes
   b. Steven Haley
   c. Donald Suthers
   d. Steve Christy

COMIC BOOK HEROES

A comprehensive list of the many comic books produced about the *Halloween* film franchise and Michael Myers.

Title	Manufacturer	Publication Date	Variant Covers
Chaos! Comics			
Untold Tales of Halloween	Chaos!	Note: Special preview ashcan issue. Only 66 ever made. Ultra rare.	
Halloween	Chaos!	November 2000	5
Halloween II: The Blackest Eyes	Chaos!	2001	4
Halloween III: The Devil's Eyes	Chaos!	2001	3
Halloween 25th Anniversary Festival			
Halloween: One Good Scare	H25 Festival	October 2003	1
Halloween Returns to Haddonfield	H25 Festival	October 2003	1
Halloween: Nightdance			
A Shape in the Void	Devil's Due Publishing	February 2008	6, plus one webstore exclusive cover.
The Silent Clown	Devil's Due Publishing	March 26, 2008	5, plus one webstore exclusive cover.

A Rainbow in One Color	Devil's Due Publishing	April 28, 2008	4, plus one webstore exclusive cover.
When the Stars Came Crashing Down	Devil's Due Publishing	May 28, 2008	3, plus one webstore exclusive cover.
The First Death of Laurie Strode			
Masks and Grotesque Figures	Devil's Due Publishing	October 17, 2008	3
Demons Tormenting Me	Devil's Due Publishing	November 23, 2008	3
The Infernal Cortege	Devil's Due Publishing	August 3, 2015	2
Single Issues			
Halloween: Autopsis	Paranormal Pictures	July 25, 2006	Note: Came in the *25 Years of Terror* DVD
Halloween: 30 Years of Terror	Devil's Due Publishing	August, 2008	4, plus one webstore exclusive cover.
Halloween Trade Paperback Vol. 1 Nightdance	Devil's Due Publishing	August 13, 2008	Note: graphic novel
Downloadable Comics (Free downloads at www.halloweencomics.com followed by the title listed in the right-hand column below)			
Halloween SAM	HalloweenComics.com		Free download at: /sam.php
Halloween White Ghost	HalloweenComics.com		Free download at:/whiteghost.php

"It's Halloween. Everyone's entitled to one good scare."
— *Sheriff Brackett (Halloween (1978))*

SCREAMING IN THE NIGHT

Answers on page 266

Questions all about Jamie Lee Curtis.

1) Jamie Lee Curtis appeared in *Halloween H20: 20 Years Later* with her mother, Janet Leigh, but what was the first film they appeared in together?

2) Jamie Lee Curtis was portraying Lt. Barbara Duran on what TV series when she landed her breakthrough role in *Halloween* (1978)?

3) Jamie Lee Curtis's character Hannah Miller worked at *Chicago Monthly* magazine with Marty Gold (Richard Lewis) in what early 1990s sitcom for which she won a Golden Globe Award?
   a. *Something So Right*   c. *Anything But Love*
   b. *Blind Justice*   d. *Hearts Afire*

4) Jamie Lee Curtis gave her phone number to future husband Christopher Guest's agent after she saw him in Rolling Stone Magazine dressed as his character from which film?
   a. *This is Spinal Tap*   c. *A Few Good Men*
   b. *The Princess Bride*   d. *The Three Musketeers*

5) What company took out an insurance policy on Jamie Lee Curtis's legs while she was doing commercials for their product?
   a. L'Eggs Pantyhose
   b. Frederick's of Hollywood
   c. Activia Yogurt
   d. Nair Hair Removal Cream

6) Upon the death of husband Christopher Guest's father, Jamie Lee Curtis gained which title of nobility?
   a. Duchess of Earl
   b. Countess Rugen
   c. Baroness Haden-Guest of Saling in the County of Essex
   d. Lady Mistress Guest of Wallace

7) Jamie Lee Curtis actually holds a U.S. Patent for which item?
   a. Hands-free baby carrier
   b. Mesh baby stroller cover
   c. Disposable diaper with a baby wipe pocket
   d. Nightlight that projects the solar system on the ceiling

8) Which of these is not a book written by Jamie Lee Curtis?
   a. *The Star Quilt*
   b. *Is There Really a Human Race?*
   c. *My Mommy Hung the Moon: A Love Story*
   d. *Big Words for Little People*

PRIMAL SCREAM
Answers on page 267

Match these Jamie Lee Curtis characters to the film or TV show they appeared on.

1) *Trading Places*
2) *N.C.I.S.*
3) *Rudolph the Red-Nosed Reindeer & the Island of Misfit Toys*
4) *Terror Train*
5) *Beverly Hills Chihuahua*
6) *Scream Queens*
7) *Freaky Friday*
8) *Prom Night*
9) *True Lies*
10) *A Fish Called Wanda*

    a. Helen Tasker
    b. Samantha Ryan
    c. Ophelia
    d. Dean Cathy Munsch
    e. Aunt Viv
    f. Kim
    g. Queen Camilla
    h. Wanda Gershwitz
    i. Alana
    j. Tess Coleman

DEMON SPEEDING

During the opening credits of *Halloween H20: 20 Years Later*, a newspaper article is shown. The subject of the article is Laurie Strode's car accident and faked death. This is the full text of the article that can be seen. Please note that "1968" is NOT a typo; it is what the article mistakenly says.

Headline: Survivor of Halloween Murders Killed in Auto Accident

By: Mary-Austin Klein, Staff Writer

Longtime Haddonfield resident Laurie Strode, survivor of the so-called "Halloween" mass murders in 1968, was killed yesterday in an auto accident.

Police estimate Miss Strode was traveling in excess of 80 miles an hour when she failed to negotiate a curve on Highway 18 near Porterville and slammed into a tree. The posted speed limit is 45. Eyewitnesses reported the late model sedan had been driving erratically before the accident occurred.

Friends had no explanation for the reckless behavior of Miss Strode, reporting she had been "the happiest of her life" in recent weeks.

THE INVISIBLE MAN
Answers on page 268

Questions all about some unseen characters.

1) What is the name of the boy that Laurie Strode has a crush on in the original *Halloween* (1978)?

2) What is the name of Annie's boyfriend in the original *Halloween* (1978)?

3) What is the name of Ronny's girlfriend/wife that he talks to multiple times on the phone in *Halloween H20: 20 Years Later?*
   a. Pearl   c. Laverne
   b. Kensi   d. Shirl

4) Alice tells Sally that her parents went to visit which of her relatives in *Halloween II* (1981)?
   a. Aunt Ruby   c. Cousin Kennedy
   b. Uncle Oswald   d. Niece Jackie

5) What is the name of the babysitter that had to cancel on the Carruthers family, leaving Rachel to have to babysit Jamie in *Halloween 4: The Return of Michael Myers?*
   a. Angie Benjamin   c. Susan Pierce
   b. Alice Franklin   d. Jesse Alan

6) Who owns the Quick Food Mart that the kids steal the three cases of beer from in *Halloween 5: The Revenge of Michael Myers?*
   a. Mr. Jones   c. Mr. Millevue
   b. Mr. Anderson   d. Mr. Casey

7) What was the name of the random person that Earl and his posse shoot, thinking it was Michael Myers, in *Halloween 4: The Return of Michael Myers?*
   a. Ben Meeker   c. Ted Hollister
   b. Enos Strate   d. Randy Hickey

8) What is the name of paramedic Budd's brother in *Halloween II* (1981)?
   a. Mark   c. Tommy
   b. Doyle   d. Johnny

9) What is the name of the girls' French teacher in the 2007 *Halloween* remake?
   a. Mr. Clouseau   c. Mr. Dickson
   b. Mr. Byner   d. Mr. LeClare

10) In an added TV scene of the original *Halloween* (1978), Lynda tells Laurie that she thinks the creep following them in the mask is who?
   a. Tony Todd   c. Tony Bell
   b. Ben Tramer   d. Scott Todd

11) Who sends a Marshall to get Dr. Loomis and escort him back to Smith's Grove Sanitarium because he is causing a panic in *Halloween II* (1981)?
   a. Mayor of Haddonfield
   b. Sheriff Brackett
   c. Dr. Terrance Wynn
   d. Governor of Illinois

12) Who was Harry Grimbridge supposed to meet for dinner on October 21, but never showed up or called, in *Halloween III: Season of the Witch*?
   a. Linda Challis
   b. Minnie Blankenship
   c. Holly Henderson
   d. Harper Eden

13) Richard and Darlene Carruthers were going to have dinner at whose house in *Halloween 4: The Return of Michael Myers*?
   a. The Fox family's house
   b. The Tramer family's house
   c. The Fallbrooks family's house
   d. The Van Der Klok family's house

FOR THE FIRST TIME

From the very start, the *Halloween* franchise has seen the film debuts of many actors, some memorable and many never to be heard from again. This is a comprehensive list of those who have made their debuts in a *Halloween* film.

ACTOR	CHARACTER	NOTES
Halloween (1978)		
Jamie Lee Curtis	Laurie Strode	Had a few TV roles before getting her big break in the original *Halloween*. She instantly became THE Scream Queen.
John Michael Graham	Bob Simms	His only film role ever.
Nancy Stephens	Nurse Marion Chambers	Had done nothing but TV work for 13 years prior.
Brent LePage	Lonnie Elamb	His only film role ever.
Tony Moran	Michael Myers	His next film role wouldn't come until 2011.
Will Sandin	Young Michael Myers	His only film role ever.

Halloween II (1981)		
Lance Guest	Jimmy	
Ana Alicia	Janet Newhall	Had some TV roles for four years prior.
Dana Carvey	Reporter's Assistant	He can be seen wearing a red flannel shirt, a vest jacket, and a hat while talking to a blonde reporter at around the 22 minute and 19 second mark of the film.
Adam Gunn	Young Michael Myers	His only film role ever. Had done TV for four years prior.
Nichole Drucker	Young Laurie Strode	Her only film role ever.
Anne Bruner	Alice	
Halloween III: Season of the Witch		
Jadeen Barbor	Betty Kupfer	Her only film role ever.
Brad Schacter	Little Buddy Kupfer	His next film role wouldn't come until 1990.
Wendy Wessberg	Teddy	Her only film role ever.

Halloween 4: The Return of Michael Myers		
Danielle Harris	Jamie Lloyd	She had two small TV roles prior.
Jeff Olson	Richard Carruthers	Had only done TV prior.
Leslie L. Rohland	Lindsey	Her only film role ever.
Erik Preston	Young Michael Myers	His next film role wouldn't come until 2012 in *Among Friends*, Danielle Harris's solo directorial debut.
Karen Alston	Darlene Carruthers	*Halloween 4* and *5* are her only film roles.
Halloween 5: The Revenge of Michael Myers		
Jeffrey Landman	Billy Hill	His only film role ever.
Tamara Glynn	Samantha Thomas	She had only appeared on TV prior.
Wendy Kaplan	Tina Williams	She had only appeared on TV prior.
Harper Roisman	Mountain Man	Even though he was 80 years old at the time, it was his film debut.

Halloween: The Curse of Michael Myers		
Paul Rudd	Tommy Doyle	Although the film *Clueless* was released first, this was filmed first.
Marianne Hagan	Kara Strode	Had done only TV prior.
Davin Gardner	Danny Strode	He has only been in one film since.
Janice Knickrehm	Mrs. Blankenship	Even though she was 70 at the time, this was her film debut.
Halloween H20: 20 Years Later		
Josh Hartnett	John Tate	
Jodi Lyn O'Keefe	Sarah Wainthrope	She had only appeared in one TV show prior.
Larisa Miller	Claudia	Has only done one film and some TV since.
Emmalee Thompson	Casey	Her only film role ever.
Halloween: Resurrection		
Marisa Rudiak	Nurse Phillips	Her only film role ever.

"All they took was a Halloween mask, rope, and a couple of knives."
— *Sheriff Brackett (Halloween (1978))*

DREAM POLICE

Answers on page 269

Match these law enforcement and security personnel to the proper statements.

1) Night watchman at Haddonfield General Hospital in *Halloween II* (2009) dream sequence

2) Deputy left to protect Jamie in Judith Myers's room in *Halloween 5: The Revenge of Michael Myers*

3) Took Angel Myers to a hospital in an adjoining county after her mother committed suicide in the *Halloween* remake (2007).

4) Spent most of his time talking on the phone with his girl, Shirl.

5) Father of babysitter Susan; found dead in the police station in *Halloween 4: The Return of Michael Myers*

6) Security guard at Haddonfield Memorial Hospital in *Halloween II* (1981)

7) Ate a Mega Flakey Crème Donut out of a vending machine

8) Was killed in the police station explosion at the end of *Halloween 5: The Revenge of Michael Myers*

9) Killed Ben Tramer after hitting him with his car

a. Lee Brackett

b. Buddy

c. Deputy Pierce

d. Willie

e. Charlie Bloch

f. Patrolman #3

g. Mr. Garrett

h. Ronny

i. Ben Meeker

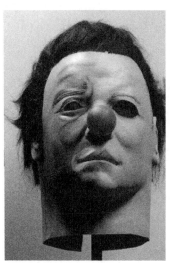

Evil Emmet - This is a custom mask which blends
the Emmett Kelly mask that was almost used with
the Michael Myers mask
(Photo courtesy: www.handiboy.com)

DOCTOR, DOCTOR

Answers on page 269

Questions all about Donald Pleasence.

1) Donald Pleasence starred alongside Frank Langella and Laurence Olivier in what 1979 horror film?

2) In what film did Donald Pleasence portray music producer B.D. Hoffler of Big Deal Records?

3) As Professor Fowler, who is being forced into retirement after 50 years of teaching, Donald Pleasence is visited by ghosts of his former students, who show him he made a difference before he can commit suicide in an episode of what TV series?

4) Donald Pleasence portrayed a villain named Ernst Stavro Blofeld in which James Bond film?
   a. *Octopussy*
   b. *Thunderball*
   c. *You Only Live Twice*
   d. *A View to a Kill*

5) Donald Pleasence was cast to be in John Carpenter's *The Thing* but had to back out due to a scheduling conflict. His role of Blair was then given to what actor?
   a. Kurt Russell   c. Richard Masur
   b. Wilford Brimley   d. Donald Moffat

6) In what other two films not part of the *Halloween* franchise did Donald Pleasence portray a character with the name Loomis?
   a. *Alone in the Dark*
   b. *Into the Darkness*
   c. *Innocent Bystanders*
   d. *Prince of Darkness*

7) Donald Pleasence portrayed Victor Frankenstein in a film that included which of Victor's relatives in the title?
   a. *Father Alphonse Frankenstein*
   b. *Great Aunt Tilly*
   c. *Sister Mary Olyphant*
   d. *Brother William Frankenstein*

8) Donald Pleasence's *Halloween* co-star Kyle Richards and her sister, Kim, appeared in what other film alongside Pleasence?
   a. *Meatballs II*
   b. *Assault on Precinct 13*
   c. *Return to Witch Mountain*
   d. *Escape to Witch Mountain*

"Maybe they're not going to have Halloween next year."
— Betty Kupfer (Halloween III: Season of the Witch)

THINGS THAT MAKE YOU GO HMMM
Answers on page 270

Questions all about some unusual facts having to do with some *Halloween* franchise cast members.

1) Michael Flynn (Deputy Pierce, Part 4) served on a mission with the Church of Jesus Christ of Latter Day Saints in France from 1966-1969, alongside what losing U.S. Presidential candidate?
   a. Al Gore
   b. Walter Mondale
   c. John Kerry
   d. Mitt Romney

2) Matthew Walker (Spitz, Part 5) left Hollywood to attend which of the following places?
   a. M.I.T.
   b. Clown College
   c. Oxford University
   d. Seminary School

3) After giving up acting, Brad Schacter (Little Buddy, Part 3) went on to become what?
   a. Surgeon
   b. Airline pilot
   c. Professor
   d. Rabbi

4) J.C. Brandy (Jamie Lloyd, Part 6) plays guitar in a band named Lo-Ball, which features which actress from an N.C.I.S. TV show on lead vocals?
   a. Daniela Ruah
   b. Pauley Perrette
   c. Renee Felice Smith
   d. Sasha Alexander

DIE, DIE MY DARLING

Answers on page 270

Questions all about some details of different kills in the films.

1) What item was used by Michael to kill Lynda in the original *Halloween* (1978)?
   a. Beer can
   b. Phone cord
   c. Knife
   d. Judith Myers's tombstone

2) What did Michael put over Paul's head after killing and hanging him in the 2007 *Halloween* remake?
   a. Potato sack   c. Jack-o-lantern
   b. Umpire's mask   d. Football helmet

3) What does Michael Myers use to kill Nurse Wynn while she sits with him in the 2007 *Halloween* remake?
   a. Fork   c. Cafeteria tray
   b. Drinking glass   d. His bare hands

4) What item was used to kill Jimmy in *Halloween H20: 20 Years Later*?
   a. Hockey stick   c. Machete
   b. Hockey puck   d. Ice skate

5) What was the name of the first person we see killed in *Halloween II* (1981)?
   a. Nancy
   b. Alice
   c. Amanda
   d. Sally

6) Who does Michael Myers kill using an aluminum baseball bat in the 2007 *Halloween* remake?
   a. Ronnie
   b. Bobby
   c. Ricky
   d. Steve

7) Who was hit and killed by a police car in *Halloween II* (1981)?
   a. Mr. Garrett
   b. Bud Doyle
   c. Mr. Roarke
   d. Ben Tramer

8) Who was the first person killed by Michael Myers by means of electrocution?
   a. Willie
   b. Craig
   c. Bucky
   d. Thurman

9) What did Michael Myers use to hang and kill Deputy Charlie Bloch in *Halloween 5: The Revenge of Michael Myers*?
   a. Emergency ladder
   b. Lamp cord
   c. Curtain
   d. Hair dryer cord

10) What does Michael finally use to kill the guard Ismael Cruz during his breakout from the hospital in the director's cut of the 2007 *Halloween* remake?
   a. Desk chair   c. Television
   b. Shovel   d. Safe

11) At the start of *Halloween: Resurrection,* we learn that Laurie Strode didn't decapitate Michael Myers at the end of *Halloween H20: Twenty Years Later,* but instead killed who?
   a. A firefighter   c. A police officer
   b. A paramedic   d. A coroner

12) Who was killed by having two fingers driven into their eyes and then having their skull pulled apart by a robot assassin?
   a. Buddy Kupfer   c. Harry Grimbridge
   b. Bella Challis   d. Conal Cochran

13) Who was decapitated with a sickle after trying to fight back against Michael Myers using a pitchfork she had pulled from her just-killed boyfriend, Spitz?
   a. Tina   c. Rachel
   b. Samantha   d. Pamela

14) What is the name of the first person we see Michael Myers kill in the 2007 *Halloween* remake?
   a. Wesley Rhoades   c. Dusty Rhodes
   b. Corey Matthews   d. Jack Anderson

CELLULOID HEROES
Answers on page 271

Match these films that were seen within the *Halloween* films to their proper questions.

1) What movie is being watched by Laurie, Tommy, and Lindsey in the original *Halloween* (1978)?

2) What Bela Lugosi film can be seen in Rob Zombie's 2007 remake of *Halloween*?

3) What film was on in the Elrod household when Michael Myers comes in to get a knife in *Halloween II* (1981)?

4) What movie is on Jimmy's television when Marion comes in and finds him dead in *Halloween H20: 20 Years Later*?

5) What movie is on the television in Sarah and Molly's dorm room in *Halloween H20: 20 Years Later*?

6) What movie was playing in the Horrorthon that Dr. Daniel Challis is forced to watch in *Halloween III: Season of the Witch*?

7) What film is being watched by Mrs. Blankenship in *Halloween: The Curse of Michael Myers*?

a.   *The Phantom of the Opera* (1925)

b.   *White Zombie* (1932)

c.   *The Thing From Another Plane*t (1951)

d.   *Plan 9 From Outer Space* (1959)

e.   *Night of the Living Dead* (1968)

f.   *Halloween* (1978)

g.   *Scream 2* (1997)

Halloween H20: 20 Years Later
German DVD cover jack-o-lantern

DEAD MAN'S PARTY

Answers on page 271

Questions all about some of the Halloween parties in the films.

1) Where was the big Halloween party being held in *Halloween 5: The Revenge of Michael Myers?*
   a) Greene Farm
   b) Empire Farm
   c) Higgins Farm
   d) Tower Farm

2) What is the name of the big party the girls go to in *Halloween II* (2009)?
   a) Phantom Jam
   b) Haddonfield Bash
   c) Halloween Jam
   d) Shadow Rave

3) Myles is persuaded to go to whose Halloween party instead of sitting home to watch Dangertainment in *Halloween: Resurrection?*
   a) John Simpson
   b) Randy Hundley
   c) Mickey Stearns
   d) Howard Jackson

4) Who hosted the rally/party at the Junior College in *Halloween: The Curse of Michael Myers?*
   a) Larry Taylor
   b) Barry Simms
   c) Frank Hoffstetler
   d) Henry Carson

BEHIND THE SCENES
Answers on page 271

1) Who composed the now iconic *Halloween* theme music?

2) Which *Halloween* film was actually released on Friday the 13th?

3) How much did actress Jamie Lee Curtis make for her role of Laurie Strode in the original *Halloween* (1978)?
   a. $50 a day
   b. $800
   c. $2000 a week
   d. $8000

4) In the original script for *Halloween 4: The Return of Michael Myers*, what was Jamie Lloyd's name?
   a. Christine
   b. Angel
   c. Brittany
   d. Danielle

5) Who provided the voice of Darlene Carruthers in *Halloween 5: The Revenge of Michael Myers*?
   a. Ellie Cornell
   b. Wendy Kaplan
   c. Kathleen Kinmont
   d. Tamara Glynn

6) Since they were filming during the spring in California, the crew had to buy which of the following to try and make it seem more like Illinois on Halloween?
   a. Coats
   b. Fake icicles
   c. Paper leaves
   d. Fake snow machine

7) Which Halloween film was originally going to be titled *Halloween: The Homecoming?*
   a. *Halloween 5: The Revenge of Michael Myers*
   b. *Halloween: Resurrection*
   c. *Halloween: The Curse of Michael Myers*
   d. *Halloween II* (1981)

8) What was the fluid that came out of the robots' mouths in *Halloween III: Season of the Witch?*
   a. Chocolate sauce
   b. Orange juice
   c. Milk mixed with food coloring
   d. Green slime obtained from Nickelodeon

9) The musical score for the original *Halloween* (1978) was credited to what group, made up by the actual composer, John Carpenter?
   a. The Bowling Green Philharmonic
   b. The Haddonfield Heights
   c. The Draculs
   d. The Sloths

10) Of those that portrayed Laurie, Annie, and Lynda in the original and the remake, which two actresses were the only teenagers, despite their characters all being teens?
   a. Jamie Lee Curtis and Scout Taylor-Compton
   b. P.J. Soles and Kristina Klebe
   c. Nancy (Loomis) Keyes and Danielle Harris
   d. Jamie Lee Curtis and Danielle Harris

11) Which of these was almost the title of *Halloween: The Curse of Michael Myers?*
    a. *Halloween: Origins*
    b. *Halloween 666: The Origin of Michael Myers*
    c. *Halloween 6: Samhain*
    d. *Halloween 6: Family Curse*

12) In *Halloween II* (1981), when Alice is talking on the phone with her friend Sally, who is providing the voice of Sally?
    a. Debra Hill
    b. Kelly Curtis (Jamie Lee's older sister)
    c. Nancy Stephens
    d. Nancy (Loomis) Keyes

13) Who provided the announcer's voice for the Silver Shamrock commercials in *Halloween III: Season of the Witch?*
    a. John Carpenter
    b. Dick Warlock
    c. Tommy Lee Wallace
    d. Charles Cyphers

14) How much was Donald Pleasence paid for his approximately 18 minutes of on-screen time, which kept him on set for five days?
    a. $10,000
    b. $20,000
    c. $25,000
    d. $50,000

15) *Halloween 5: The Revenge of Michael Myers* was released on October 13, 1989 and was the #2 movie in the U.S. during its opening weekend; what film beat it out by just over $7 million for its opening weekend?
   a. *Look Who's Talking* c. *The Little Mermaid*
   b. *Back to the Future II* d. *Ghostbusters II*

16) Which extra bit of wardrobe did Jamie Lee Curtis have to wear for *Halloween II* (1981)so that she would appear the same as she did in the original film three years earlier?
   a. Braces   c. Prosthetic nose
   b. Contact lenses d. Wig

17) Actor Donald Pleasence admitted to director John Carpenter that the only reason he took the role was because his daughter, Angela, loved what other Carpenter film?
   a. *Dark Star*   c. *Assault on Precinct 13*
   b. *Eyes of Laura Mars* d. *They Live*

18) John Carpenter named the character Michael Myers after which of the following?
   a. Someone who bullied him in high school
   b. Co-writer Debra Hill's first boyfriend
   c. Distributor of *Assault on Precinct 13*
   d. An actor from the film *Invasion of the Bodysnatchers*

19) What was the original title of *Halloween H20: 20 Years Later* going to be?
   a. *Halloween III: Aftercare*
   b. *Halloween: Origins*
   c. *Halloween 7: The Revenge of Laurie Strode*
   d. *Halloween: Homeward Bound*

20) Which *Halloween* film's score was supplemented with Marco Beltrami's scores from *Scream*, *Scream 2*, and *Mimic* after producers were unhappy with the original score presented by John Ottman?
   a. *Halloween: Resurrection*
   b. *Halloween 5: The Revenge of Michael Myers*
   c. *Halloween: The Curse of Michael Myers*
   d. *Halloween H20: 20 Years Later*

21) There is a well-known behind-the-scenes photo of Nick Castle with the Michael Myers mask pulled up high on his head. He is pretending the mask is drinking a can of what beverage?
   a. Budweiser   c. Dr. Pepper
   b. Coca-Cola   d. Pepsi

22) There is a well-known behind-the-scenes photo of Dick Warlock in full Michael Myers costume holding a can of what beverage?
   a. Budweiser   c. Dr. Pepper
   b. Coca-Cola   d. Pepsi

(SHE'S) SEXY + 17

Many actors in the *Halloween* film franchise portray characters that are supposed to be a certain age – quite a few of them 17 years old. The actors, more often than not, are a much different age than their characters, though. Here is a list of some of the main characters.

Actor - Age	Character - Age
Halloween **(1978)**	
Jamie Lee Curtis - 19	Laurie Strode – 17
Nancy (Loomis) Keyes - 28	Annie Brackett - 17
P.J. Soles - 28	Lynda Van Der Klok - 17
Sandy Johnson - 24	Judith Myers – 15
Halloween 4: The Return of Michael Myers	
Danielle Harris - 10	Jamie Lloyd - 8
Ellie Cornell - 24	Rachel Carruthers - 17
Kathleen Kinmont - 23	Kelly Meeker - 17
Sasha Jenson - 23	Brady - 17
Halloween 5: The Revenge of Michael Myers	
Tamara Glynn - 20	Samantha Thomas - 18
Matthew Walker - 20	Spitz - 18
Wendy Kaplan - 23	Tina Williams - 18

Halloween: The Curse of Michael Myers	
J.C. Brandy - 19	Jamie Lloyd - 15
Marianne Hagan - 29	Kara Strode - 22
Paul Rudd - 26	Tommy Doyle – Tommy's age is uncertain. He is 17 years plus whatever his age was in the original *Halloween*. That age is under 13, based on the fact that Laurie says Tommy's classmate Lonnie Elamb will never make it out of 6th grade, which implies they are in the 6th grade or lower. This means Tommy could be 30 at most and probably no less than 26 or 27.

Halloween H20: 20 Years Later	
Josh Hartnett - 19	John Tate - 17
Michelle Williams – 17	Molly Cartwell - 17
Jodi Lyn O'Keefe - 19	Sarah Wainthrope - 17
Adam Hann-Byrd - 16	Charlie Deveraux - 17

Halloween: Resurrection	
The ages of their characters are unknown. They are all college-aged students, though Myles is a few years younger and perhaps in high school.	
Bianca Kajlich - 25	Sara Moyer
Katee Sackhoff - 22	Jenna Danzig
Sean Patrick Thomas - 31	Rudy Grimes
Ryan Merriman - 18	Myles Barton

Halloween (2007)	
Scout Taylor-Compton - 18	Laurie Strode - 17
Danielle Harris - 30	Annie Brackett - 17
Kristina Klebe - 28	Lynda Van Der Klok - 17
Hannah Hall - 23	Judith Myers - 16
Daeg Faerch - 12	Michael Myers - 10
Halloween II (2009)	
Angela Timbur - 27	Harley David – 18-19
Brea Grant - 27	Mya Rockwell – 18-19

"To make Michael Myers frightening, I had him walk like a man, not a monster."
– John Carpenter

THE KIDS AREN'T ALRIGHT
Answers on page 273

Questions all about the younger children in the films.

1) Laurie Strode is babysitting what child in the original *Halloween* (1978) as well as in the 2007 remake?
   a. Billy Franklin   c. Bobby Hill
   b. Tommy Doyle   d. Jason Miller

2) Annie is babysitting which child in the original *Halloween* (1978) as well as in the 2007 remake?
   a. Holly Richards   c. Samantha Gallo
   b. Kenzi Anderson   d. Lindsey Wallace

3) What is the name of the little boy who lived in the Myers house and survived a battle with Michael in *Halloween: The Curse of Michael Myers*?
   a. Ben Tramer   c. Al Myers
   b. Danny Strode   d. Andy Wallace

4) What name did Tommy Doyle give to Jamie Lloyd's son in *Halloween: The Curse of Michael Myers*?
   a. Reggie   c. Steven
   b. Paul   d. Michael

5) Who told Tommy Doyle that the Myers house was haunted in the original *Halloween* (1978)?
   a. Ronnie Eggert
   b. Lonnie Elamb
   c. Lanny Poffo
   d. Danny Faison

6) What had happened to the little boy whose mother is taking him to the emergency room as Laurie Strode arrives at the hospital in *Halloween II* (1981)?
   a. Stepped on a nail
   b. Cut his hand with a knife
   c. Put his eye out with a slingshot
   d. Bit into a razor blade

7) What is the name of the little boy that gives Jamie Lloyd flowers and a bracelet in *Halloween 5: The Revenge of Michael Myers*?
   a. Billy Hill
   b. Franklin Hardy
   c. Jack Anderson
   d. Michael Smith

A WHISPER TO A SCREAM
Answers on page 273

Questions all about Danielle Harris.

1) In the early 1990s, Danielle Harris portrayed Molly Tilden in a handful of episodes of what TV sitcom?

2) Danielle Harris provided the voice of Debbie for six seasons of what Nickelodeon animated series?

3) Danielle Harris portrays Bruce Willis's daughter, Darian Hallenbeck, in what 1991 action film?

4) Danielle Harris portrayed the girlfriend in a violent relationship who winds up committing suicide in a music video for the song "The Bleeding" by what band?
   a. Disturbed
   b. Shinedown
   c. Three Days Grace
   d. Five Finger Death Punch

5) In what horror film was Danielle Harris's character Tosh Guaneri brutally murdered while her roommate laid in the bed across the room?
   a. *Shiver*
   b. *Urban Legend*
   c. *Hallow's Eve*
   d. *The Victim*

6) Danielle Harris is a member of what group, alongside Rick McCallum, R.A. Mihailoff, Kane Hodder, and others?
   a. Hollywood Horror Tours
   b. Horror Actor's Hall of Fame
   c. Hollywood Ghost Hunters
   d. Horror Charities Association

7) What is the subtitle of the 2009 Danielle Harris horror movie, *Blood Night*?
   a. *The Legend of Victor Crowley*
   b. *The Legend of Melissa Crandell*
   c. *The Legend of Marybeth*
   d. *The Legend of Mary Hatchet*

8) In what 2010 horror film does Danielle Harris portray a vampire named Belle?
   a. *The Ward*
   b. *Stake Land*
   c. *My Soul to Take*
   d. *The Crazies*

9) Danielle Harris co-directed what 2008 film with fellow *Halloween 4* and *5* star Ellie Cornell and *A Nightmare on Elm Street* star Heather Langenkamp, which featured other *Halloween* franchise alums J.C. Brandy, Kathleen Kinmont, and P.J. Soles?
   a. *Crank Call*
   b. *Hang Up*
   c. *Prank*
   d. *Wrong Number*

10) What was the name of the show hosted by Danielle Harris's character Maria Sanchez in the film *Cyrus: Mind of a Serial Killer?*
a) *Real Crime*   c) *Murder Tales*
b) *Last Steps*   d) *Killer Stories*

11) What was the title of Danielle Harris's 2012 solo directorial debut?
a. *Among Friends*   c. *The Dinner Party*
b. *One Lonely Night*   d. *Whodunit?*

12) In the film *Don't Tell Mom the Babysitter's Dead,* Danielle Harris's character Mellissa played for what Little League baseball team?
a. Kings   c. Barons
b. Royals   d. Monarchs

13) In a *Freaky Friday*-like TV movie titled *Wish Upon a Star,* Danielle Harris portrays Hayley Wheaton. She wishes to trade places with her older, popular sister Alexia, who is portrayed by what future *Grey's Anatomy* star?
a. Ellen Pompeo   c. Katherine Heigl
b. Chyler Leigh   d. Sandra Oh

"He'll never die."
— *Jamie Lloyd (Halloween 5: The Revenge of Michael Myers)*

SILENT SCREAM
Answers on page 274

Match Danielle Harris's co-star with the film they appeared in together.

1) Kane Hodder
2) Glen "Kane" Jacobs
3) Sylvester Stallone
4) Steven Seagal
5) Christina Applegate
6) Felissa Rose
7) Lacey Chabert
8) Lance Henriksen
9) Robert Patrick
10) David Faustino

a. *Ghost of Goodnight Lane*
b. *Camp Dread*
c. *Hatchet II*
d. *Marked for Death*
e. *See No Evil 2*
f. *Killer Bud*
g. *Cyrus: Mind of a Serial Killer*
h. *Daylight*
i. *Don't Tell Mom the Babysitter's Dead*
j. *The Black Waters of Echo's Pond*

THE CURSE

This is the Runic symbol for Thorn.

Tommy Doyle (as read by actor Paul Rudd) had a narration during the opening credits of *Halloween: The Curse of Michael Myers*; this is the full text of his narration.

"When Michael Myers was six years old, he stabbed his sister to death. For years, he was locked up in Smith's Grove Sanitarium, but he escaped. And suddenly, Halloween became another word for mayhem! One by one, he killed his entire family, until his nine-year-old niece, Jamie Lloyd, was the only one left alive. Six years ago, Halloween night, Michael and Jamie vanished. Many people believed them dead, but I think that someone hid them away. Someone who keeps Michael, protects him, tries to control him. And if there's one thing I know, you can't control evil. You can lock it up, you can burn it and bury it and pray that it dies, but it never will. It just rests a while. You can lock your doors and say your prayers at night, but the evil's out there waiting. And maybe, just maybe, it's closer than you think!"

In the producer's cut of *Halloween: The Curse of Michael Myers*, the narration was instead read by Dr. Loomis (as read by actor Donald Pleasence). This is the full text of his narration.

"When Michael Myers was six years old, he stabbed his sister to death. For years, he was locked up, locked away in Smith's Grove Sanitarium, but he escaped. And suddenly, Halloween was another word for mayhem! He needed to wipe out his entire family. He struck them down at night and always on Halloween. The police tried everything to stop him. He overcame them all, and disappeared. The world thought him dead, but I, I wasn't sure. I wasn't sure that Michael Myers had died."

PAC-MAN FEVER

Answers on page 274

Wizard Video Games created a *Halloween* game for the Atari 2600 in 1983. The player became the babysitter character and had to save the children from a knife-wielding killer. The characters, however, were not named – not even the killer.

1) How many points did you get for each child you saved in the game?
   a. 100   c. 500
   b. 250   d. 675

2) How many lives did you get at the start of every game?
   a. 3   c. 5
   b. 4   d. 6

3) What symbol is used at the top of the screen to indicate the number of remaining lives you have?
   a. Knife   c. Mask
   b. Jack-o-lantern   d. Heart

4) What happened when the killer got you or one of the children in the game?
   a. Character screamed
   b. Character died and floated off-screen
   c. Character was decapitated
   d. Character was dragged off by the killer

5) What did the killer do if you picked up an unidentifiable weapon and got him with it?
   a. He tore off his mask.
   b. He threw a knife at you.
   c. He laughed at you.
   d. He ran away.

6) To save on the cost of the game later in production, how did Wizard Video begin labeling the cartridges?
   a. A piece of tape with "Halloween" written on it in marker
   b. A sticker of a jack-o-lantern with creepy carvings
   c. A blurry picture of Michael Myers
   d. An image of a mental institution

7) What happened when the killer appeared on-screen?
   a. The *Halloween* theme music played.
   b. The babysitter screamed.
   c. The background turned orange.
   d. The children yelled "Trick or treat!"

DOWN ON THE CORNER
Answers on page 275

Questions all about some locations in the films.

1) In what city was the Illinois State Hospital located in the original *Halloween* (1978)?

2) The elementary school that Michael Myers breaks into in *Halloween II* (1981) is located on what road?
   a. Elm Street
   b. Reservoir Road
   c. Dusk Avenue
   d. Lincoln Avenue

3) In what Illinois town do the opening scenes of *Halloween H20: 20 Years Later* take place?
   a. Lanford
   b. Aurora
   c. Oakdale
   d. Langdon

4) Laurie Strode is walking in a daze down what street at the opening of *Halloween II* (2009)?
   a. Carpenter Street
   b. Hill Street
   c. Floyd Street
   d. Carr Avenue

5) Where does the ambulance transferring Michael Myers crash just south of in *Halloween 4: The Return of Michael Myers*?
   a. Polecat Creek
   b. Holmdel Creek
   c. Mill Creek
   d. Sand Pond

6) Who lives at 4946 Cypress Pond Road in
   Halloween H20: 20 Years Later?
   a. Virginia Alves   c. Marion Whetington
   b. Keri Tate   d. Norma Watson

7) What other two Illinois cities were listed on the
   sign when Dr. Loomis was trying to get a ride to
   Haddonfield in *Halloween 4: The Return of Michael
   Myers?*
   a. Peoria and Aurora
   b. Springfield and Bowling Green
   c. Naperville and East Nigma
   d. Eaton and Chicago

8) Where did an eyewitness say they saw a large man
   carrying a body away from a car accident and into
   a small shack in *Halloween II* (2009)?
   a. Turkey Hill Road   c. Eagle Road
   b. Trout Avenue   d. Winchester Avenue

9) What can be found at the street address 1605
   Shady Lane in the *Halloween* movie franchise?
   a. Haddonfield Memorial Hospital
   b. Smith's Grove Sanitarium
   c. Haddonfield Community College
   d. Uncle Meat's Java Hole

10) What is the street address of the Brackett house
    in *Halloween II* (2009)?
    a. 13 Apple Tree   c. 15 Cherrywood
    b. 14 Pinewood   d. 16 Gin Blossom

SLEEPING WITH THE TELEVISION ON
Answers on page 276

Match these *Halloween* franchise cast members to the character they played and the TV show where they appeared.

1) Troy Evans
2) Bianca Kajlich
3) Tyra Banks
4) Beau Starr
5) Jodi Lyn O'Keefe

6) Cliff Emmich
7) Bill Fagerbakke
8) Kathleen Kinmont
9) Silas Weir Mitchell
10) William Forsythe

a. Lt. Harding Welsh
b. Digger
c. Cheyenne Phillips
d. Sgt. Pepper
e. Cassidy Bridges

f. Leslie Burton
g. Jackie Ames
h. Monroe
i. Dauber Dybinski
j. Candy Man

i. *China Beach*
ii. *Happy Days*
iii. *Coach*
iv. *Due South*
v. *Grimm*

vi. *Renegade*
vii. *Undateable*
viii. *Nash Bridges*
ix. *John Doe*
x. *Fresh Prince of Bel-Air*

"Oh, we've got a psychotic serial killer in the family who loves to butcher people on Halloween, and I just thought it in bad taste to celebrate."
— John Tate (Strode) (Halloween H20: 20 Years Later)

GOING BACK TO CALI

Answers on page 276

Questions all about *Halloween H20: 20 Years Later.*

1) What is the name of the security guard at Hillcrest Academy High School?
   a. James   c. Ronny
   b. Sam   d. Jack

2) In what year was Hillcrest Academy High School established?
   a. 1848   c. 1939
   b. 1922   d. 1978

3) Hillcrest Academy High School students go on a trip to what location in *Halloween H20: 20 Years Later?*
   a. Yosemite   c. Grand Canyon
   b. San Francisco d. Sacramento

4) John Tate's father sent a card for his 17th birthday how many months late?
   a. 4 months   c. 2 months
   b. 1 month   d. 3 months

5) Who does Will Brennan shoot in *Halloween H20: 20 Years Later?*
   a. Keri/Laurie
   b. Molly
   c. John Tate
   d. Ronny

6) What does Charley drop into the garbage disposal right before Michael kills him in *Halloween H20: 20 Years Later?*
   a. Corkscrew
   b. *Back to the Future* keychain
   c. Class ring
   d. Contact lens

7) According to the coroner's van at the end of *Halloween H20: 20 Years Later*, in what town is Hillcrest Academy located?
   a. Summer Glen
   b. Springfield
   c. Tinton Falls
   d. Winterfell

8) What does security guard Ronny dream of becoming in *Halloween H20: 20 Years Later?*
   a. Rapper
   b. Federal agent
   c. Writer of erotic fiction
   d. TV host

10-31

MASKS

PUT YOUR DEATH MASK ON
Answers on page 277

1) How much did the original James T. Kirk mask that was converted to be used as Michael Myers's mask in *Halloween* (1978) cost?

2) Where did they get the mask to use in *Halloween II* (1981)?

3) As *Halloween II* (1981) was supposed to be the final appearance of Michael Myers, which cast member was allowed to keep the mask after filming was done?

4) What famed mask maker took on the job of supplying the masks used in *Halloween III: Season of the Witch* after he had turned down the chance to make a mask for the original *Halloween* (1978)?

5) Which of the three main masks used in *Halloween III: Season of the Witch* had to be created from scratch, while the other two were simply variations of masks already offered by the company supplying them?

6) The mask that Michael Myers wore while in Mikey's car in *Halloween 5: The Revenge of Michael Myers* was originally supposed to be of which U.S. President?

7) When deciding what mask to use for the original *Halloween* (1978), the first option was a mask of which clown, which was deemed too creepy?
   a. Ronald McDonald
   b. Chuckles
   c. Emmett Kelly
   d. Clarabell

8) Which sequel had four different masks made for it, had to have many scenes reshot due to criticism of the masks, and also used a CGI mask put in frame-by-frame for some scenes that could not be reshot?
   a. *Halloween 4: The Return of Michael Myers*
   b. *Halloween 5: The Revenge of Michael Myers*
   c. *Halloween: The Curse of Michael Myers*
   d. *Halloween H20: 20 Years Later*

Don Post 1975 Captain
James T. Kirk / William
Shatner Replica
*(Photo courtesy: Kevin S.
King)*

Halloween (1978)
Young Michael
Clown Mask
*(Photo courtesy: Kevin S.
King)*

Halloween (1978)
*(Photo courtesy: Chris
Morgan)*

Halloween II (1981)
*(Photo courtesy: Chris
Morgan)*

Halloween II (1981)
Ben Tramer
(Photo courtesy: handiboy.com)

Halloween III: Season of the Witch
Silver Shamrock
Skull
(Photo courtesy: Kevin S. King)

Halloween III: Season of the Witch
Silver Shamrock
Witch
(Photo courtesy: Kevin S. King)

Halloween III: Season of the Witch
Silver Shamrock
Jack-o-lantern
(Photo courtesy: Kevin S. King)

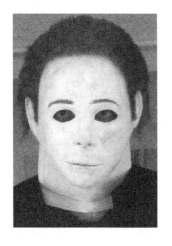

Halloween 4: The Return of Michael Myers (Photo courtesy: Ben Fallaize / Father Phantom Studio - This mask was cast from the "Hero" mask made for the film.*)*

Halloween 5: The Revenge of Michael Myers (Photo courtesy: Jeff Paskach / Midwest Masks N Mayhem)

Halloween 5: The Revenge of Michael Myers "Brute" mask worn by both Mikey and Michael Myers in the film. *(Photo courtesy: Kevin S. King)*

Halloween: The Curse of Michael Myers (Photo courtesy: Chris Morgan)

Halloween H20: 20 Years Later (Photo courtesy: Ben Fallaize / Father Phantom Studio – This mask was cast from a backup mask made for production of the film.)

Halloween: Resurrection (Photo courtesy: Chris Morgan)

Halloween (2007)
Young Michael
Clown Mask
(Photo courtesy: Kevin S. King)

Halloween (2007)
(Photo courtesy: Ben Fallaize / Father Phantom Studio)

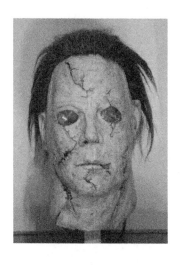

Halloween II (2009)
(Photo courtesy: handiboy.com)

BAD MEDICINE

Answers on page 277

Questions all about some medical professionals in the films.

1) What is the name of the nurse that is telling the story of Laurie to Nurse Philips (who just started at the hospital) in *Halloween: Resurrection*?
   a. Nurse Waters
   c. Nurse Ocean
   b. Nurse Rivers
   d. Nurse Wells

2) What were the names of the two paramedics that took Laurie to the hospital in *Halloween II* (1981)?
   a. Jimmy and Budd
   c. Budd and Doyle
   b. Billy and Ted
   d. Bob and Vinny

3) How much does Laurie Strode's therapist charge per hour in *Halloween II* (2009)?
   a. $50
   c. $250
   b. $100
   d. $300

4) What is the name of the head nurse at Haddonfield Memorial Hospital in *Halloween II* (1981)?
   a. Mary Lands, RN
   b. Virginia Alves, RN
   c. Della Warren, RN
   d. Carolina Anderson, RN

5) Which nurse attempts to leave the hospital and get the sheriff, only to find that the tires on all the cars in the parking lot have been slashed, in *Halloween II* (1981)?
   a. Julia Jackson, RN
   b. Janet Anderson, RN
   c. Jill Franco, RN
   d. Jeri Janeway, RN

6) What was the name of the nurse that paramedic Budd was dating in *Halloween II* (1981)?
   a. Gale Weathers, RN
   b. Brittany Rainey, RN
   c. Haley Storm, RN
   d. Karen Rainey, RN

7) Which two men are in charge of Smith's Grove Sanitarium in the 2007 *Halloween* remake?
   a. Dr. Koplenson and Morgan Walker
   b. Chuck Anderson and Frank Williams
   c. Dr. Wynn and Morgan Jackson
   d. William Francis and Alan Jefferson

"Evil hiding among us is an ancient theme."
— John Carpenter

THE WILD AND THE YOUNG
Answers on page 278

Match these young couples to the statement that best describes them.

1) While having sex in a barn, he was killed with a pitchfork; she fought back with that same pitchfork, but ultimately lost her head.

2) She makes it clear that she needs dinner and a few drinks before anything fun can happen; unfortunately for him he has a bit of trouble with the corkscrew.

3) For this couple, a bit of roleplay didn't end so well when Michael stepped in and offered her a beer from under the sheets.

4) These two decided to do the couples costume thing and dress as Frankenstein and the Bride of Frankenstein.

5) This couple were the main characters in Ronny's erotic fiction story.

6) They had a date for the big Halloween party, but her date wound up being with Michael Myers instead, who borrowed her boyfriend's car.

7) When her school funding falls through, this couple decides on a stay-cation instead of going away with their friends.

8) Even though one stuttered and the other was a mute for the better portion of the film, this couple managed to communicate better than the rest.

9) This couple only had an online relationship, but in the end they finally meet face to face.

10) The only couple to attempt to have sex in *Halloween II* (1981). It doesn't work out as things get a bit overheated.

11) This couple was never seen together in the original *Halloween* (1978); of course when we do see them in the remake, it doesn't go well at all as he winds up wearing a jack-o-lantern and she barely survives.

a. Sarah and Charlie   g. Lynda and Bob
b. Karen and Budd   h. Tim and Beth
c. Samantha and Spitz   i. Jamie and Billy
d. Molly and John   j. Annie and Paul
e. Sara and Myles   k. Tina and Mikey
f. Lawrence and Tonya

THEY'RE COMING TO TAKE ME AWAY
Answers on page 278

Match these hospitals with their proper questions.

1) What is the name of the sanitarium in which Laurie is being held in *Halloween: Resurrection?*

2) What is the name of the maximum security facility that Michael Myers is being kept in at the beginning of *Halloween 4: The Return of Michael Myers?*

3) Laurie Strode is taken to what medical facility in *Halloween II* (1981)?

4) Laurie Strode, Annie Brackett, and Dr. Sam Loomis are all treated at what hospital in *Halloween II* (2009)?

5) What is the name of the hospital where Michael Myers spends most of his life after killing his sister Judith?

   a. Haddonfield General Hospital
   b. Smith's Grove Sanitarium
   c. Grace Andersen Sanitarium
   d. Haddonfield Memorial Hospital
   e. Ridgemont Federal Sanitarium

POP LIFE

Answers on page 279

Questions all about things pulled from the world of pop culture.

1) The three comic books Laurie reads the titles of in the original *Halloween* (1978) were fake; the comics that were used in the scene were actually from what comic book series?
   a. *Dick Tracy*   c. *The Avengers*
   b. *Howard the Duck*   d. *Archie*

2) Tommy Doyle was named after a character in which Alfred Hitchcock film?
   a. *The Man Who Knew Too Much*
   b. *Rear Window*
   c. *Suspicion*
   d. *Dial M for Murder*

3) What advertising mascot can be seen on the counters in both Penney's restaurant and Earl's bar in *Halloween 4: The Return of Michael Myers*?
   a. Spuds MacKenzie   c. The Energizer Bunny
   b. The Domino's   d. A Budweiser
      Pizza Noid   Clydesdale

4) Who was the other guest on *The Newman Hour* besides Dr. Loomis in *Halloween II* (2009)?
   a. Wayne Knight   c. Chris Hardwick
   b. Weird Al Yankovic d. Jenny McCarthy

5) What type of laptop does Sara have in *Halloween: Resurrection*?
   a. Hewlett Packard   c. Toshiba Satellite
   b. Dell   d. Apple iBook

6) What brand of laundry detergent is used by the Wallace family in the original *Halloween* (1978)?
   a. Tide   c. Fab
   b. Wisk   d. Cheer

7) Where was Rachel going to take Jamie for ice cream after school instead of trick-or-treating?
   a. Friendly's   c. Freddy's Ice Cream
   b. Carvel   d. Dairy Queen

8) What brand of popcorn does Annie make in the original *Halloween* (1978)?
   a. Jiffy Pop   c. Orville Redenbacher's
   b. Jolly Time   d. Butterkist

9) The wife of which *The Brady Bunch* actor portrayed the dead waitress in Penney's restaurant in *Halloween 4: The Return of Michael Myers*?
   a. Barry Williams   c. Christopher Knight
   b. Robbie Rist   d. Mike Lookinland

10) Big Joe Grizzly quotes which Paul Newman film when Michael Myers is confronting him while in the bathroom in the *Halloween* remake (2007)?
   a. *Butch Cassidy and the Sundance Kid*
   b. *Cool Hand Luke*
   c. *The Color of Money*
   d. *The Sting*

11) The *Family Guy* episode "Tom Tucker: The Man and His Dream," reveals that Tucker once portrayed Michael Myers under what stage name?
   a. George P. Wilbur
   b. Tommy Lee Wallace
   c. Dick Warlock
   d. Don Shanks

12) Annie says she will make Lindsey watch six straight hours of whose horror movie show?
   a. Dr. Dementia
   b. Elvira, Mistress of the Dark
   c. Count Floyd
   d. The Phantom of the Opry

13) In the Woody Allen film *Broadway Danny Rose*, a movie theater marquee proclaimed which *Halloween* film was playing?
   a. *Halloween*
   b. *Halloween II*
   c. *Halloween III: Season of the Witch*
   d. *Halloween 4: The Return of Michael Myers*

14) What is the ironic name of Keri/Laurie's assistant in *Halloween H20: 20 Years Later*?
   a. Marion
   b. Laurie
   c. Jamie
   d. Norma

15) In Keri/Laurie's class, they are talking about the characters Victor and Elizabeth from what story?
   a. *Dracula*
   b. *To Kill a Mockingbird*
   c. *Wuthering Heights*
   d. *Frankenstein*

16) Laurie Strode had a poster of what Expressionist painter, whose works include human figures wearing grotesque masks, on her bedroom wall in *Halloween* (1978)?
   a. James Ensor
   b. Jean-Luc Kirk Sisko
   c. Pierre Paulus
   d. Roger Raveel

17) What does Sara use to communicate with Deckard while she is trying to escape from Michael Myers in *Halloween: Resurrection*?
   a. Cell phone
   b. Skype
   c. Palm pilot
   d. Satellite phone

18) What famous person did Sheriff Brackett bring up at dinner while discussing Starving Marvin in *Halloween II* (2009)?

a. Marvin Hagler   c. Lee Marvin
b. Marvin Gaye   d. Marvin Hamlisch

19) Weird Al Yankovic mentions which movie character during his appearance on *The Newman Hour* after Dr. Loomis references Michael Myers in *Halloween II* (2009)?

a. Shrek   c. Austin Powers
b. Wayne Campbell   d. Dr. Evil

20) P.J. Soles was originally asked to portray Keri/Laurie's assistant Norma, which would have been ironic as Soles had previously portrayed Norma in which other film?

a. *Psycho II*
b. *Carrie*
c. *Christine*
d. *The Texas Chainsaw Massacre II*

VALLEY GIRL

Answers on page 280

Questions all about P.J. Soles.

1) John Carpenter wanted P.J. Soles to be in *Halloween* (1978) after seeing her in which other film?

2) P.J. Soles appeared in which other Rob Zombie film?

3) What was P.J. Soles's character's name in the film *Rock 'n' Roll High School*?
   a. Angel Dust
   b. Riff Randell
   c. Kate Rambeau
   d. Erica Ramone

4) What do the initials P.J. stand for in P.J. Soles's name?
   a. Polly Jessica
   b. Penelope Judy
   c. Pamela Jayne
   d. Phyllis June

5) In the early 1980s, P.J. Soles appeared in which two films that revolved around the military?
   a. *Private Benjamin* and *Stripes*
   b. *Apocalypse Now* and *The Deer Hunter*
   c. *Heartbreak Ridge* and *Hamburger Hill*
   d. *Full Metal Jacket* and *Platoon*

ROCK 'N' ROLL HIGH SCHOOL
Answers on page 280

Questions all about schools in the films.

1) What is the name of the high school where Keri/Laurie works as Headmistress in *Halloween H20: 20 Years Later?*
   a. Valley View Academy
   b. Brookline Academy
   c. Raritan Bay Academy
   d. Hillcrest Academy

2) Characters in *Halloween: The Curse of Michael Myers* attend what institute of higher learning?
   a. University of Illinois – Haddonfield
   b. Haddonfield Junior College
   c. Haddonfield Polytechnic School
   d. Community College of Haddonfield

3) Charley says that he attended what college while setting up the cameras for the reality show in *Halloween: Resurrection?*
   a. Manhattan School of Film
   b. Castle Rock Film Institute
   c. J. Hughes Film School of Shermer, Illinois
   d. Long Beach State

4) What college was attended by some characters in *Halloween: Resurrection*?
   a. Haddonfield University
   b. Haddonfield Community College
   c. Thorn College
   d. University of Illinois – Smith's Grove

5) In what year was Haddonfield Junior College founded?
   a. 1949
   b. 1957
   c. 1963
   d. 1978

Halloween II replica mask of the scene after Laurie shoots Michael and we briefly see the blood on the mask. *(Photo courtesy: handiboy.com)*

(O, WHAT A) LUCKY MAN

Answers on page 280

Questions all about Malcolm McDowell.

1) Malcolm McDowell is credited as the performer of what song in the cult-classic film *A Clockwork Orange*?
   a. "Raindrops Keep Falling On My Head"
   b. "Amazing Grace"
   c. "Singin' in the Rain"
   d. "Jailhouse Rock"

2) Malcolm McDowell was once married to what well-known actress?
   a. Mary Steenburgen
   b. Candice Bergen
   c. Madeline Kahn
   d. Helen Mirren

3) Malcolm McDowell appeared in which music video for the band Slipknot?
   a. "Killpop"
   b. "Snuff"
   c. "Psychosocial"
   d. "Duality"

4) In the film *Time After Time*, Malcolm McDowell's character H.G. Wells pursues what criminal through time?
   a. John Wayne Gacy   c. Theo Durrant
   b. H.H. Holmes   d. Jack the Ripper

5) Malcolm McDowell received death threats after one of his characters killed which popular character in a movie?
   a. Kenny McCormick
   b. Captain James T. Kirk
   c. God
   d. Yoda

6) Malcolm McDowell's character in *A Clockwork Orange*, Alex DeLarge, enjoys the music of which composer?
   a) Fryderyk Chopin
   b) Wolfgang Amadeus Mozart
   c) Ludwig van Beethoven
   d) Johann Sebastian Bach

7) Malcolm McDowell portrays vampire hunter Eddie Van Helsing in what 2009 comedy horror?
   a. *Bite*
   b. *Suck*
   c. *Blood*
   d. *The Darkness*

8) Malcolm McDowell does a series of rather funny commercials with James Earl Jones for what cell phone carrier?
   a. Sprint
   b. AT&T
   c. U.S. Cellular
   d. Verizon

SINGIN' IN THE RAIN
Answers on page 281

Match these Malcolm McDowell characters to the films in which they appeared.

1) Father Murder
2) Satan
3) Paul Gallier
4) Daniel Linderman
5) Principal Gibbons
6) Stanton Infeld
7) Dr. Tolian Soran
8) Dr. Miles Langford
9) Mr. Roarke
10) Scamboli

    a. *Star Trek: Generations*
    b. *Franklin & Bash*
    c. *Fantasy Island*
    d. *31*
    e. *Cat People*
    f. *Pinocchio 3000*
    g. *Suing the Devil*
    h. *Easy A*
    i. *Heroes*
    j. *Class of 1999*

"Martians could land on Ben's doorstep and all he'd do is spit once and get himself a shotgun."
— Earl *(Halloween 4: The Return of Michael Myers)*

DRESSED TO KILL

Answers on page 281

Questions all about some clothes worn in the films.

1) The cover of which KISS member's solo album appears on Laurie Strode's t-shirt in *Halloween II* (2009)?

2) Due to the small budget, the actors wore their own clothes; Jamie Lee Curtis got her entire wardrobe for *Halloween* (1978) for under $100 at what store?
   a. Sears
   b. JC Penney
   c. Macy's
   d. Wal-Mart

3) Danny and his Uncle Tim Strode are seen wearing t-shirts that say what on them in *Halloween: The Curse of Michael Myers*?
   a. I'm With Stupid
   b. Barry Kicks Ass
   c. Trick or Treat
   d. Haddonfield Huskies

4) What band is on Laurie Strode's shirt when she gets sick at dinner in *Halloween II* (2009)?
   a. Faster Pussycat
   b. White Zombie
   c. Fastway
   d. Black Flag

5) What does it say on Kelly Meeker's t-shirt when she answers the door for trick-or-treaters in *Halloween 4: The Return of Michael Myers*?
   a. Handle With Care
   b. Cops Do It By The Book
   c. Angel
   d. Boo!

6) The hoodie worn by Scout Taylor-Compton in the remake *Halloween* (2007) was actually part of which cast member's clothing line, called "Total Skull"?
   a. Danielle Harris
   b. Her own (Scout Taylor-Compton)
   c. Sheri Moon Zombie
   d. Malcolm McDowell

"DIE!"
— Michael Myers (Halloween II (2009))

THE ROOTS OF ALL EVIL

A list of all of Michael Myers's family from the different incarnations of the *Halloween* series.

Character/Appearance	Actor/Actress	Notes
Mother		
Mrs. Myers B: 12-13-1926, D: 1-3-1965		
Remake: B: 1954, D: 1992		
Unnamed Mrs. Myers / *Halloween* (1978), *Halloween II* (1981)		Uncredited and unnamed in the films.
Edith Myers / Novelization 1979		Author Dennis Etchison used the pseudonym Curtis Richards to write the book.
Audrey Myers / Chaos Comics		Michael Myers's middle name is Audrey.
Deborah Myers / *Halloween* (2007), *Halloween II* (2009)	Sheri Moon Zombie	Director Rob Zombie originally wanted his wife Sheri to portray Lynda. In the end, he chose her as Michael's mother due to her height, which helped explain Michael's adult height in the film.

Father		
Mr. Myers B: 1-10-1925, D: 1-3-1965		
Peter Myers/ *Halloween* (1978)	George O'Hanlon, Jr.	
Donald Myers / Novelization 1979		
Sister		
Judith Margaret Myers B: 11-10-1947, D: 10-31-1963		
Remake: B: 1974, D: October 31, 1990		
Halloween (1978)	Sandy Johnson	In the original, Judith was given the same birthdate as co-writer Debra Hill.
Halloween (2007)	Hanna R. Hall	
Sister		
Laurie Strode B: 1961, 4-6 Timeline D: 11-30-1987		
***H20* Timeline: D: 10-31-2001**		
Remake Timeline: B: 1990, D: 10-31-2009		
Cynthia Myers / Laurie Strode		
Halloween (1978), *Halloween II* (1981), *Halloween H20: 20 Years Later, Halloween: Resurrection*	Jamie Lee Curtis	It is believed that Curtis only returned for *Resurrection* because of contractual obligation.
Halloween II (1981)	Nichole Drucker	Young Laurie
Angel Myers / Laurie Strode		
Halloween (2007), *Halloween II* (2009)	Scout Taylor-Compton, Sydnie Pitzer, Myla Pitzer, Stella Altman	Sydnie and Myla Pizter and Stella Altman all played the infant Angel Myers.

Niece Jamie Lloyd B: 1980, D: 10-30-1995		
Halloween 4: The Return of Michael Myers, Halloween 5: The Revenge of Michael Myers	Danielle Harris	
Halloween: The Curse of Michael Myers	J.C. Brandy	The studio and Harris could not come to an agreement, and she was also not happy with the direction of the film, which is why she was ultimately replaced by Brandy.
Great Nephew Steven Lloyd B: 10-30-1995		
Halloween: The Curse of Michael Myers		
Nephew John Tate B: 08-1981		
Halloween H20: Twenty Years Later	Josh Hartnett	This was Hartnett's film debut.

WE ARE YOUNG
Answers on page 282

Questions all about some *Halloween* franchise cast members as child actors in other films and TV shows.

1) Joseph Gordon-Levitt's (Jimmy, *H20*) first recurring TV role was actually a dual role of David and Daniel Collins in the remake of what long-running late 1960s show?
   a. *The New Munsters*
   b. *The New Leave It to Beaver*
   c. *Dark Shadows*
   d. *Forever Knight*

2) Daryl Sabara (Wesley Rhoades, Remake) starred as Juni Cortez in what Robert Rodriguez film franchise?
   a. *From Dusk Till Dawn*
   b. *Spy Kids*
   c. *Sin City*
   d. *Machete*

3) Thomas Ian Nicholas (Bill, Part 8) starred as Henry Rowengartner in *Rookie of the Year*. What Major League Baseball team did he pitch for in the film?
   a. New York Yankees
   b. Chicago White Sox
   c. New York Mets
   d. Chicago Cubs

4) Skyler Gisondo (Tommy Doyle, Remake) portrayed Young Shawn on what USA Network original series?
   a. *Psych*   c. *Covert Affairs*
   b. *Monk*   d. *Suits*

5) Ryan Merriman (Myles Barton, Part 8) portrayed the younger version of the main character on what late 1990s TV series?
   a. *J.A.G.*
   b. *The Pretender*
   c. *Early Edition*
   d. *Hercules: The Legendary Journeys*

6) Kim Darby (Debra Strode, Part 6) at age 16 portrayed a character named Miri in an episode of which 1960s hit TV series?
   a. *Bonanza*   c. *Batman*
   b. *The Twilight Zone*   d. *Star Trek*

7) Adam Hann-Byrd (Charlie, *H20*) portrayed Jodie Foster's son in which 1991 film at just nine years old?
   a. *Nell*   c. *Little Man Tate*
   b. *The Accused*   d. *The Silence of the Lambs*

8) Adam Weisman's (Steve, Remake) film debut was as Young Bud in what 1996 comedy?
   a. *Encino Man*   c. *Bio-Dome*
   b. *Son-In-Law*   d. *Jury Duty*

9) Hanna Hall (Judith Myers, Remake) portrayed Young Jenny Curran in what hit film from 1994?
   a. *Pulp Fiction*
   b. *Forrest Gump*
   c. *True Lies*
   d. *Interview with the Vampire*

10) Michelle Williams (Molly Cartwell, *H20*) portrayed the younger version of Natasha Henstridge's character Sil in what 1995 horror film?
   a. *Species*
   b. *The Prophecy*
   c. *Candyman: Farewell to the Flesh*
   d. *Leprechaun 3*

11) Skyler Gisondo (Tommy Doyle, Remake) portrayed Bryan Pearson, the son of which of the Blue Collar Comedy stars in a TV sitcom?
   a. Jeff Foxworthy
   b. Larry the Cable Guy
   c. Bill Engvall
   d. Ron White

12) Courtney Gains (Jack Kendall, Remake) made his film debut as Malachai in what 1984 horror film?
   a. *Silent Night, Deadly Night*
   b. *A Nightmare On Elm Street*
   c. *C.H.U.D.*
   d. *Children of the Corn*

DIRTY LAUNDRY

Answers on page 282

Questions all about some media outlets and their reporters/hosts in the films.

1) What was the name of the radio call-in show featured in *Halloween: The Curse of Michael Myers?*
   a. Shock Talk
   b. Back Talk
   c. Night Chat
   d. Midnight Caller

2) What is the name of the reporter that we see interview both Dr. Samuel Loomis and Big Lou in *Halloween II* (2009)?
   a. Holly West
   b. Molly North
   c. Marie South
   d. Shelly Eastwood

3) What was the name of the reporter doing the special news bulletins in *Halloween II* (1981)?
   a. Robert Campbell
   b. Anderson Shell
   c. Robert Monday
   d. Alan Branson

4) What were the call letters of the TV station airing the special news bulletins in *Halloween II* (1981)?
   a. WPIX
   b. KPAX
   c. KTEL
   d. WWAR

5) Which television channel's news does Holly West work for in *Halloween II* (2009)?
   a. News 18 KPOW
   b. News 18 WESP
   c. News 18 WPKW
   d. News 18 WASH

6) What is the name of the host of the radio call-in show Back Talk, which is featured in *Halloween: The Curse of Michael Myers*?
   a. Barry Simms
   b. Frank Mimms
   c. Sam Hain
   d. Alan Sam

Halloween 4: The Return of Michael Myers – Michael's escape in bandages replica mask, and Jamie Lloyd's clown with blood splatter replica mask.
(Photo courtesy: Kevin S. King)

I CAN'T LIVE WITHOUT MY RADIO
Answers on page 283

Questions all about music in the films.

1) What song is played at the beginning and the end of *Halloween II* (1981)?

2) What song is playing when we see Deborah Myers dancing at work in the 2007 *Halloween* remake?

3) A music video for what song is seen multiple times while Laurie is dreaming about being chased by Michael at the hospital in *Halloween II* (2009)?

4) What band is playing on the radio before John turns it off during their party after they hear a loud crash in *Halloween H20: 20 Years Later*?
   a. White Zombie
   b. Creed
   c. The Misfits
   d. Pink Floyd

5) What song is playing on the radio while Lynda and Bob are in the Myers house in the 2007 *Halloween* remake?
   a. "Don't Fear the Reaper"
   b. "House of Pain"
   c. "Takin' Care of Business"
   d. "Two Steps Behind"

6) What was the name of the band that played at the Phantom Jam party in *Halloween II* (2009)?
   a. Powerman 5000
   b. The Crypt Kickers
   c. The Cemetery Gates
   d. Captain Clegg and The Night Creatures

7) What song was playing on the radio in Floyd's truck as he, Jazlean, and Sherman headed out to confront Michael Myers for being on their land?
   a. "Sharp Dressed Man" by ZZ Top
   b. "What's Your Name?" by Lynyrd Skynyrd
   c. "Devil's Food" by Alice Cooper
   d. "Flirtin' with Disaster" by Molly Hatchet

8) Which song, which was remade by Metallica, was playing in Laurie Strode's car when she angrily drove from Annie's house to Mya's house after learning that her true identity was Angel Myers?
   a. "Die, Die My Darling" by The Misfits
   b. "Whiskey in the Jar" by Thin Lizzy
   c. "Am I Evil?" by Diamond Head
   d. "Stone Cold Crazy" by Queen

GOD GAVE ROCK AND ROLL TO YOU II
Answers on page 283

Name the song . . .

1) played at the start of the 2007 *Halloween* remake.

2) playing as the Kupfer family arrives in their RV at the hotel in *Halloween III: Season of the Witch*.

3) turned on by Mya while at Uncle Meat's Java Hole in *Halloween II* (2009).

4) Judith Myers is listening to in her headphones in the 2007 *Halloween* remake.

5) playing on the radio in Mikey's car when he is parked outside of the Quick Food Mart in *Halloween 5: The Revenge of Michael Myers*.

6) being played as Big Joe Grizzly pulls into the truck washing station in the 2007 *Halloween* remake.

7) playing at the end of *Halloween II* (2009) as Laurie lay dying next to Michael and Dr. Loomis.

8) playing as Annie and Paul have sex on the couch in the 2007 *Halloween* remake.

9) playing as Harley awaits Wolfie's return to the van in *Halloween II* (2009).

10) playing after the coroner's van crashes and Michael escapes in *Halloween II* (2009).

11) playing as Michael returns to Haddonfield after his escape in the 2007 *Halloween* remake.

   a. "Only Women Bleed" by Alice Cooper

   b. "Baby I'm Yours" by Barbara Lewis

   c. "Mr. Sandman" by The Chordettes

   d. "Kick Out the Jams" by MC5

   e. "Do the Boogaloo" by Quango & Sparky

   f. "The Things We Do For Love" by 10CC

   g. "Don't Fear the Reaper" by Blue Oyster Cult

   h. "Tom Sawyer" by Rush

   i. "God of Thunder" by KISS

   j. "Love Hurts" by Nazareth

   k. "I Just Want to Make Love to You" by Foghat

I GOT A NAME

Answers on page 284

Questions all about some nicknames and aliases.

1) Annie's nickname on her cheerleading jacket in the 2007 *Halloween* remake is what?
   a. Daddy's Girl   c. Hot Stuff
   b. Shortcake   d. Munchkin

2) What is Lynda's nickname on her cheerleading jacket in the 2007 *Halloween* remake?
   a. Cherry Bomb   c. Kiss of Death
   b. Blackheart   d. Space Ace

3) What does Danny call the man he hears talking to him at night in *Halloween: The Curse of Michael Myers*?
   a. Mr. Cash   c. Voice Man
   b. The Boogeyman   d. Sandman

4) What does Michael Myers call his younger sister, who turns out to be Laurie Strode, in the 2007 *Halloween* remake?
   a. Angel Baby   c. Pebbly Poo
   b. Baby Boo   d. Sissy

5) Sara knows Myles Barton, the freshman that tells her he is a graduate student and who helps her with computer support in *Halloween: Resurrection*, by what name?
   a. Becker   c. Davis
   b. Bart   d. Deckard

PHOTOGRAPH

Answers on page 284

Questions all about some posters, photos, and signs seen hanging in the films.

1) A poster of what rock star can be seen on Laurie and Annie's bathroom wall in *Halloween II* (2009)?
   a. Ozzy Osbourne   c. Ace Frehley
   b. Alice Cooper   d. Scott Ian

2) A crumpled-up photo of whom is hung above Laurie's bed in *Halloween: Resurrection*?
   a. Tommy Doyle   c. Jamie Lloyd
   b. Michael Myers   d. John Tate

3) A painting of which U.S. president can be seen hanging on the wall of the Myers house in the 2007 *Halloween* remake?
   a. Bill Clinton   c. Ronald Reagan
   b. John F. Kennedy   d. Barack Obama

4) Laurie has a poster of which infamous figure on the wall above her bed in *Halloween II* (2009)?
   a. Charles Manson   c. Ed Gein
   b. John Wayne Gacy   d. Vlad the Impaler

5) Multiple photos of which U.S. president can be seen on the wall of Penney's restaurant in *Halloween 4: The Return Of Michael Myers*?
   a. Abraham Lincoln   c. Ronald Reagan
   b. John F. Kennedy   d. George Washington

6) What is the slogan on the Big Cookie Lady sign that can be seen outside of Dale's Gas Station?
   a. Chock Full of Chips!
   b. The Cookie That Pleases!
   c. The Biggest Cookie in Town!
   d. Giant Cookies...A Real Taste Treat!

7) What does the sign above Judith Myers's bed say in the 2007 *Halloween* remake?
   a. Place Hands Here
   b. Jesus Saves
   c. Learn from your parents' mistakes; use birth control!
   d. John 3:16

8) On the wall of Uncle Meat's Java Hole, we see an iconic poster of whom, sitting on a toilet?
   a. Weird Al Yankovic
   b. Archie Bunker
   c. President Lyndon B. Johnson
   d. Frank Zappa

9) By what nickname is Michael Myers mentioned on the sign for The World Famous Rabbit in Red, home of Deborah Myers, mother of Michael Myers in *Halloween II* (2009)?
   a. The World's Most Prolific Serial Killer
   b. The Babysitter Murderer
   c. The Haddonfield Slasher
   d. The Butcher of Haddonfield

PET SOUNDS

Answers on page 285

Questions all about some animals featured in the films.

1) What type of animals were on Jamie Lloyd's pajamas in *Halloween 5: The Revenge of Michael Myers*?
   a. Dogs
   b. Cats
   c. Rabbits
   d. Dinosaurs

2) What does the coroner's van hit while taking Michael's body to the morgue at the start of *Halloween II* (2009)?
   a. Armadillo
   b. Cow
   c. Deer
   d. Wolf

3) What is the name of Michael Myers's pet rat in the 2007 *Halloween* remake?
   a. Elvis
   b. Elton
   c. Billy
   d. Stevie

Match the pets to their names:

1) Mountain Man's parrot in *Halloween 5: The Revenge of Michael Myers*

2) Wallace family dog in *Halloween* (1978)

3) Benny family dog in *Halloween II* (2009)

4) Carruthers family dog in *Halloween 4: The Return of Michael Myers*

5) Carruthers family dog in *Halloween 5: The Revenge of Michael Myers*

    a. Ivan
    b. Sundae
    c. Max
    d. Lester
    e. Tooky

"They're going to kill us. All of us! All of us!"
— Harry Grimbridge (*Halloween III: Season of the Witch*)

SEASON OF THE WITCH

Answers on page 285

Questions all about Halloween *III: Season of the Witch*.

1) What is the name of the company that makes the masks featured in *Halloween III: Season of the Witch*?

2) A five-ton blue stone disappeared from where in *Halloween III: Season of the Witch*?

3) Businesswoman Marge Gutman owns a shop in Union Square in what California city in *Halloween III: Season of the Witch*?
   a. Santa Monica
   b. San Francisco
   c. San Diego
   d. San Jose

4) Daniel and Ellie get a room at what motel in *Halloween III: Season of the Witch*?
   a. Irish Eyes Motel
   b. Shamrock Inn
   c. Rose of Shannon Motel
   d. Blarney Bed & Breakfast

5) What is the name of the bar that is across the street from the phone booth that Dr. Daniel Challis uses to call for help in *Halloween III: Season of the Witch*?
   a. Moe's Tavern on the Green
   b. Gilded Rose
   c. Danny Boy's
   d. Gary's Old Towne Tavern

6) What is the name of the town where the Silver Shamrock Novelties factory is located?
   a. Springwood   c. Santa Mira
   b. Hardesty   d. Fairvale

7) In some TV versions of Halloween *III: Season of the Witch*, Buddy Kupfer's line about "sticky toilet paper" was changed to what?
   a. Sticky paper towels
   b. Sticky dwarf toys
   c. Sticky troll dolls
   d. Sticky cigars

8) What color is the laser that shoots out at Marge Gutman when she tampers with the Silver Shamrock medallion that falls out of her son's mask in *Halloween III: Season of the Witch*?
   a. Green   c. Yellow
   b. Red   d. Blue

9) Before it became a toy factory, what was the Silver Shamrock Novelties factory in *Halloween III: Season of the Witch*?
   a. A dairy
   b. A clothing warehouse
   c. An automobile plant
   d. A bomb-making factory

10) What was the name of the bartender in the bar when Ellie comes in to talk to Daniel in *Halloween III: Season of the Witch*?
    a. Gordon
    b. Graham
    c. Charlie
    d. Joe

11) In what year was the town of Santa Mira founded in *Halloween III: Season of the Witch*?
    a. 1799
    b. 1849
    c. 1887
    d. 1946

12) What day of the week does Halloween fall on in *Halloween III: Season of the Witch*?
    a. Sunday
    b. Tuesday
    c. Thursday
    d. Saturday

13) What time is the big Silver Shamrock Novelties Halloween giveaway in *Halloween III: Season of the Witch*?
    a. 7:00P.M.
    b. 9:00P.M.
    c. 6:00P.M.
    d. 10:00P.M.

14) The demonic figure at the top of the *Halloween III: Season of the Witch* movie poster is a distorted version of which of the masks used in the film?
   a. Skull
   b. Witch
   c. Frankenstein
   d. Jack-o-lantern

15) *Halloween III*'s subtitle was taken from what writer/director's 1972 film *Season of the Witch*, also known as *Hungry Wives*?
   a. Tobe Hooper
   b. Don Siegel
   c. George A. Romero
   d. Wes Craven

Opening sequence computer graphic *Halloween III: Season of the Witch* jack-o-lantern

MISERY BUSINESS
Answers on page 286

Questions all about businesses featured in the films.

1) What was the name of the company that Laurie's father owned in the original *Halloween* (1978)?

2) What is the name of the business seen on Nurse Marion Chambers's matchbook cover in the original *Halloween* (1978)?

3) What was the name of the store that Rachel and Jamie go to for a Halloween costume?

4) What business that was broken into was located at the corner of Mission Street and Meridian Avenue in the original *Halloween* (1978)?

5) Where was Tina Williams when a bunch of police cars showed up to rescue her from trouble after Jamie has one of her visions of Michael in *Halloween 5: The Revenge of Michael Myers*?
   a. Mr. Meeker's Deli   c. Wynn's Grocery
   b. Dale's Gas Station   d. Joey B's Diner

6) What is the name of the business that owned the red pickup truck which was driven by the mechanic that Michael Myers killed for his clothes in the original *Halloween* (1978)?
   a. Balboni Garage   c. Mattingly Garage
   b. Chambliss Garage   d. Phelps Garage

7) What company runs the bus depot that serves northern Illinois in *Halloween: The Curse of Michael Myers*?
   a. Fastrip
   b. E-Z Trip
   c. QuikTrip
   d. EasyRide

8) What is the name of the bookstore where Laurie Strode buys Dr. Loomis's new book in *Halloween II (2009)*?
   a. Stacked Books
   b. Cover to Cover
   c. The Old Town Reader
   d. Buy the Book

9) What is the name of the gas station located in Santa Mira in *Halloween III: Season of the Witch*?
   a. Rafferty's
   b. Egan's
   c. Campbell's
   d. Brown's

10) What bus company owned the bus that dropped off the mysterious man dressed in black in Haddonfield in *Halloween 5: The Revenge of Michael Myers*?
   a. Kubiak Bros. Stages
   b. Musso Bros. Stages
   c. Lewis Bros. Stages
   d. Steiner Bros. Stages

154

11) When Dr. Loomis stops to use the payphone halfway between Smith's Grove and Haddonfield, what business is advertised on the billboard in the background?
   a. Libbey Glass Factory Outlet Store
   b. Patrick Clothes Factory Outlet Store
   c. Quentin Shoe Factory Outlet Store
   d. Grace Oils Factory Outlet Store

12) What is the name of the restaurant that is next to the auto body shop where Dr. Loomis stops for gas in *Halloween 4: The Return of Michael Myers*?
   a. Sheldon's
   b. Howard's
   c. Penney's
   d. Leonard's

HE'S BACK
(THE MAN BEHIND THE MASK)
Answers on page 287

Questions all about some things that cross over from the *Halloween* movie franchise and the *Friday the 13th* movie franchise.

1) What director of *Friday the 13th Part 2* and *Friday the 13th Part III* also directed a *Halloween* film?

2) Movie trailers for *Halloween: Resurrection* first appeared before screenings of which *Friday the 13th* sequel?

3) Who is the only person to portray Jason Voorhees, Michael Myers, and Leatherface on screen?
   a. Kane Hodder
   b. Ted White
   c. Richard Brooker
   d. Tom Morga

4) Who is the only actor to appear in films with Michael Myers, Jason Voorhees, and Freddy Krueger?
   a. Kyle Labine
   b. Lar Park Lincoln
   c. Will Butler
   d. Travis Van Winkle

5) Tommy Lee Wallace directed *Jason Lives: Friday the 13ᵗʰ Part VI* alumnus Vinny Guastaferro in a 1985 episode of which TV anthology series titled "Dreams for Sale," an episode which also included two other shorts directed by Wes Craven?

    a. *Masters of Horror*   c. *Tales from the Darkside*
    b. *The Twilight Zone*   d. *Tales from the Crypt*

6) Which *Halloween* franchise writer also directed the documentaries *Crystal Lake Memories: The Complete History of Friday the 13ᵗʰ* and *His Name Was Jason: 30 Years of Friday the 13ᵗʰ* , as well as *Never Sleep Again: The Elm Street Legacy* and *Scream: The Inside Story*?

    a. Daniel Farrands
    b. Michael Jacobs
    c. Tommy Lee Wallace
    d. Robert Zappia

7) Which *Friday the 13ᵗʰ* director was brought in to do additional make-up and special effects to add some blood to *Halloween 4: The Return of Michael Myers* after producers didn't think there was enough in the initial finished version?

    a. Marcus Nispel
    b. Adam Marcus
    c. Tom McLoughlin
    d. John Carl Buechler

8) What makeup specialist that worked on *Halloween H20: 20 Years Later* also worked on *Friday the 13th* Parts 3 & 5, as well as the original *A Nightmare on Elm Street* and various other Freddy Krueger productions?
   a. Tom Savini
   b. Louis Lazzara
   c. Dick Smith
   d. Greg Nicotero

9) Which make-up and effects duo not only worked on *Halloween 5*, *Friday the 13th* (Part 9), and *A Nightmare on Elm Street* (Part 5), but have also done work in *The Texas Chainsaw Massacre*, *Evil Dead*, *From Dusk Till Dawn*, and *Scream* movie franchises?
   a. Tom Savini and Taso Stavrakis
   b. John Carl Buechler and Tom McLoughlin
   c. Greg Nicotero and Robert Kurtzman
   d. Jules Bass and Arthur Rankin, Jr.

BACK FOR MORE
Answers on page 287

Many locations and place names have been reused for the *Halloween* films, or used elsewhere after being in a *Halloween* film. Here are questions all about some of these recycled locales.

1) What classic 1950s film also used the small town of Santa Mira as its setting?

2) The exterior of Lynda's house (1027 Montrose Ave, Pasadena, CA) from the original *Halloween* (1978) was later used in the opening sequence of which popular 1980s TV sitcom?
   a. *Charles in Charge*   c. *Too Close for Comfort*
   b. *Mama's Family*   d. *Family Ties*

3) The Myers house, which is now located at 1000 Mission Street in South Pasadena, California, was briefly seen in the 2008 remake of which horror film?
   a. *April Fool's Day*   c. *Prom Night*
   b. *Day of the Dead*   d. *Shutter*

4) The Vincent Drug Store where Jamie goes to buy her costume in *Halloween 4: The Return of Michael Myers* was also used in what sports-related film?
   a. *Field of Dreams*   c. *The Sandlot*
   b. *Slapshot*   d. *The Rookie*

5) What Stephen King film also used the same Vincent Drug Store setting that was used in *Halloween 4: The Return of Michael Myers*?
   a. *The Stand*
   b. *The Boogeyman*
   c. *Creepshow*
   d. *Children of the Corn*

6) The Riverview Hospital in Coquitlam, British Columbia, which was used as the Grace Anderson Sanitarium in *Halloween: Resurrection*, also served as the main setting for which Danielle Harris film?
   a. *Hatchet III*
   b. *Urban Legend*
   c. *Blood Night: The Legend of Mary Hatchet*
   d. *See No Evil 2*

7) When Laurie Strode sees Michael Myers standing outside her school in the 2007 remake, Michael is actually standing in front of the house that was used as which location in the original *Halloween* (1978)?
   a. The Myers house
   b. Nichol's Hardware store
   c. The Wallace house
   d. The Strode house

8) The additional scene of Laurie and Lynda inside Laurie's house, which was added for the TV version of *Halloween* (1978), was filmed at 1428 N. Genesee Avenue in Hollywood, California. This same house was used for exterior shots of the home of the main character from which other horror film?
   a. *A Nightmare on Elm Street*
   b. *Freddy vs. Jason*
   c. *Scream*
   d. *Scary Movie*

9) The gas station used in *Halloween III: Season of the Witch* was also used in what other John Carpenter film?
   a. *The Thing*
   b. *They Live*
   c. *Escape From New York*
   d. *The Fog*

10) The gun shop that Dr. Loomis purchases his gun from in the *Halloween* remake was previously used in which film?
   a. *Dawn of the Dead*
   b. *Shaun of the Dead*
   c. *The Dead Pool*
   d. *The Dead Zone*

DARKNESS ON THE EDGE OF TOWN

While the films were generally set in Haddonfield, Illinois, none were actually filmed in Illinois. Here are the many filming locations used in all ten films. Locations in parentheses are the real names of sites.

Halloween (1978)

Alhambra, CA

110 W. McLean Street – *Haddonfield High School interiors, Haddonfield Elementary exteriors (Garfield Elementary)*

Cynthia Street to Novelda Road – *The start of Annie and Laurie's drive. They then arrive at the hardware store.*

Altadena, CA

3900 Lincoln Avenue – *Smith's Grove Sanitarium (La Viña Hospital)*

Burbank, CA

South Parish Place to Parkside Avenue to South Keystone Street – *Route driven by Annie and Laurie from the hardware store to the Wallace and Doyle houses.*

City of Industry, CA

Brea Canyon Road and Old Ranch Road – *Phone booth used by Dr. Loomis*

Hollywood, CA

1530 N. Orange Grove Avenue – *Doyle house exteriors*

1533 N. Orange Grove Avenue – *Doyle house interiors*

1537 N. Orange Grove Avenue – *Wallace house exteriors*

1542 N. Orange Grove Avenue – *Wallace house interiors*

1428 N. Genesee Avenue – *Interior of Strode house filmed for additional scenes for the TV premiere of the film. Annie's phone call was actually filmed upstairs in the same house.*

Sierra Madre, CA

    East Sierra Madre Boulevard & Coburn Avenue –
    Cemetery scenes (Sierra Madre Pioneer Cemetery)

South Pasadena, CA

    1017 Montrose Avenue – *Sheriff and Annie Brackett's house*

    1019 Montrose Avenue – *Hedge scene*

    1027 Montrose Avenue – *Lynda Van Der Klok's house*

    964 Mission Street – *Nichol's Hardware Store (The Frame Shop)*

    709 Meridian Avenue – *Myers's house*

    1115 Oxley Street – *Strode house*

    1401 Fremont Avenue – *Haddonfield High School exteriors (South Pasadena High School)*

    Highland Street – *a car scene*

    Montrose Avenue and Oxley Street – *Modern-day Haddonfield opening shot*

    Meridian Avenue and Mission Street - *Intersection near hardware store*

    Meridian Avenue and Magnolia Street – *Street scenes*

Halloween II (1981)

Alhambra, CA
  110 W. McLean Street – *Haddonfield Elementary(Garfield Elementary)*

Hollywood, CA
  Raleigh Studios, 5300 Melrose Avenue – *Hospital fire scenes*

  1530 N. Orange Grove Avenue – *Doyle house exteriors, Michael Myers's newly-filmed fall from the balcony and Dr. Loomis on front lawn afterward.*

  1536 N. Orange Grove Avenue – *Neighbor questioning Loomis about the noise.*

Los Angeles, CA
  8711 S. Harvard Boulevard – *Haddonfield Memorial Hospital interior shots (Morningside Hospital)*

Sepulveda, CA
  1611 Plummer Street – *Haddonfield Memorial Hospital exterior shots (Veteran's Hospital)*

Sierra Madre, CA
  Kersting Court at Sierra Madre Boulevard and Baldwin Avenue – *Town Square*

South Pasadena, CA
  716 Meridian Avenue – *Elrod house*

  1845 N. Fair Oaks Avenue – *Haddonfield Memorial Hospital interior shots (Pasadena Community Hospital)*

  Magnolia Lane – *Alleyway behind the Elrod house*

  Magnolia Street and Meridian Avenue – *Intersection where Ben Tramer is killed.*

Halloween III: Season of the Witch

Loleta, CA

US Route 101/Redwood Highway –*Drive to Santa Mira*

Eel River Drive and Copenhagen Road – *"Welcome to Santa Mira" sign*

2457 Eel River Drive – *Rafferty's Gas and The Rose of Shannon Motel*

352 Main Street – *The Shamrock Store (Loleta Grocery)*

358 Main Street – *Shamrock Savings (Bank of Loleta)*

366 Main Street – *Dublin Inn*

512 Main Street – *The Gilded Rose Tavern*

281 Loleta Drive – *Silver Shamrock Novelties factory*

Los Angeles, CA

Don Post Studios factory – *Interiors of the Silver Shamrock Novelties factory that involved the making of masks.*

159 and 161 North Larchmont Boulevard – *The Omaha, Nebraska shot*

101 South Plymouth Boulevard – *The Baton Rouge, Louisiana shot*

Sierra Madre, CA

70 W. Sierra Madre Boulevard – *The bar (The Buccaneer)*

Kersting Court at Sierra Madre Boulevard and Baldwin Avenue – *Payphone Dr. Challis calls his wife from before leaving for Santa Mira; TV storefront.*

Sylmer, CA

14838 San Fernando Road – *Junkyard*

22124 Sierra Highway – *Gas Station*

11600 Eldridge Avenue – *Sierra Mesa Hospital (Pacoima Lutheran Medical Center)*

Halloween 4: The Return of Michael Myers

<u>Copperton, UT</u>
9350 West Bingham Highway – *Earl's Bar (Ore House Saloon)*

<u>Midvale, UT</u>
7696 North Main Street – *Vincent Drug store (interior shots were filmed at an unknown location in Cottonwood Heights, UT)*

<u>Ogden, UT</u>
West 12th Street/State Road 39 – *Ambulance crash site*

<u>Rush Valley, UT</u>
State Road 36 (North of intersection with State Road 73) – *Penney's Restaurant and gas station*

<u>Salt Lake City, UT</u>
400 East Capital Park Avenue – *Ridgemont Federal Sanitarium*

509 3rd Avenue – *Carruthers house*

1300 E. 700 South – *Haddonfield Elementary School (The McGillis School)*

602 2nd Avenue – *Meeker house*

300 North Canyon Road – *Park scenes where Ted Hollister is shot by Earl's gang (Memory Grove Park)*

Halloween 5: The Revenge of Michael Myers

Midvale, UT

> 7696 North Main Street – *Vincent Drug store where the man in black was dropped off*

Orem, UT

> Olmstead Junction/U.S. Route 189 – *Haddonfield Children's Clinic*

> 114 South 2250 West – *Tower Farm (Wheeler Farm)*

Salt Lake City, UT

> 509 3rd Avenue – *Carruthers house*

> 1007 1st Avenue – *Myers house*

> 89 D Street – *Quick Food Mart*

> South 200 East and East 600 South – *Dale's Gas Station*

Halloween: The Curse of Michael Myers

Los Angeles, CA
>   2301 Bellevue Avenue– *Reshoots of Smith's Grove (Queen of Angels Hospital)*

Layton, UT
>   891 Weaver Lane – *Farm used for Jamie's death scene*

Salt Lake City, UT
>   Sewage tunnels – *Underground cult scenes*
>
>   1926 Lincoln Street – *Myers/Strode house*
>
>   956 Ramona Avenue – *Mrs. Blankenship's house*
>
>   400 East Capital Park Avenue – *Smith's Grove exteriors*
>
>   1840 South 1300 East – *Haddonfield Junior College (Westminster College)*
>
>   320 12th Avenue – *Haddonfield Memorial Hospital (Primary Children's Hospital)*

Halloween H20: 20 Years Later

Calabasas, CA

   1925 Las Virgenes Canyon Road – *Highway 139 Northern California rest stop (Malibu Creek State Park)*

La Puente, CA

   Main Street – *Summer Glen town square*

   15819 Main Street – *Restaurant where Keri and Will have lunch*

   15834 Main Street – *Store that Charlie shoplifts a bottle of wine from*

Los Angeles, CA

   4940 Melrose Hill Street.– *Jimmy's house*

   4946 Melrose Hill Street.– *Marion's house*

   1923 Micheltorena Street.– *Hillcrest Academy (Canfield-Moreno Estate)*

Halloween: Resurrection

Los Angeles, CA
  1923 Micheltorena Street.– *Hillcrest Academy (Canfield-Moreno Estate)*

Coquitlam, British Columbia, Canada
  2601 Lougheed Highway– *Grace Anderson Sanitarium (Riverview Hospital)*

Vancouver, British Columbia, Canada
  2329 West Mall – *Haddonfield University (University of British Columbia)*

  2400 Kingsway– *2400 Motel*

  4881 Mackenzie Street– *The Richest Rags*

Halloween (2007)

Altadena, CA:

2184 North Lake Avenue – *Haddonfield Elementary interiors (Eliot Middle School)*

2400 Fair Oaks Avenue – *Haddonfield Cemetery (Mountain View Cemetery)*

2560 Fair Oaks Avenue – *Haddonfield Char Broiled Burger (Fair Oaks Char Broil Burger)*

Castaic, CA

31557 Castaic Road – *Truck wash*

31602 Castaic Road – *Rabbit in Red Lounge (Country Girl Saloon)*

Los Angeles, CA

2215 South Harvard Boulevard– *Myers house kitchen scenes*

2218 South Harvard Boulevard– *Myers house; Strode house interiors*

4730 Crystal Springs Drive, Griffith Park– *Wesley's death*

855 North Vermont Avenue– *Webster Hall (Los Angeles College campus theater building)*

6045 York Boulevard– *Haddonfield Police Department (Los Angeles Police Historical Society Museum)*

Sepulveda, CA

1611 Plummer Street – *Haddonfield Memorial Hospital exterior shots (Veteran's Hospital)*

South Pasadena, CA

1110 Glendon Way– *Myers house exteriors and some interiors*

1020 El Centro Street– *Haddonfield Elementary (South Pasadena School District Administration Building)*

1002 Highland Street– *Strode house*

1100 Oxley Street– *Haddonfield High School, Big Joe Grizzly bathroom scene (South Pasadena Library)*

1937 and 1960 La Franca Avenue– *Doyle house*

Replica of the original Myers house in *Halloween* (1978).
You can get more information about this house in Hillsborough, North Carolina and even find out how you can visit the house (by appointment or during advertised events only) on their web site at:
www.myershousenc.com
(Photo courtesy: Kenny Caperton/The Myers House NC)

Halloween II (2009):

Atlanta, GA:

> 3315 Peachtree Road – *Hotel where Loomis speaks (International Continental Hotel)*

Covington, GA:

> Clark Street to Floyd Street from the intersection with Monticello to a little beyond the intersection with Elm Street – *Laurie's zoned-out walk at the start.*

> 14567 State Highway 36 – *Haddonfield General Hospital exteriors*

> 2166 Conyers Street SW – *Myers house*

> 1113 Floyd St. NE – *The Old Town Reader bookstore (now part of Real Louisiana's Off the Square, which was next door to it in the film)*

Madison, GA:

> 144 Academy Street – *Uncle Meat's Java Hole (Dog Ear Books at the time, now Madison Markets – Antiques & Interiors)*

> 384 Hancock Street – *Sheriff Brackett's office/ Police Station exteriors (Morgan County Court House)*

Newborn, GA:

> 1981 Broughton Road – *Brackett house*

> Highway 142 – *Laurie's drive from Brackett house to therapy and Uncle Meat's*

> 4169 Highway 142 and Church Street – *Phantom Jam locale; the church in the background during the girls' arrival is at the end of Church Street (Newborn Fertilizer Company warehouse)*

> Highway 142 and Pennington Road (7 miles south of Newborn) – *The Rabbit in Red Lounge (Highway 142 Bar & Grill)*

EAT IT

Answers on page 288

Questions all about some food items in the films.

1) Which pizza topping does Budd the Paramedic hate in *Halloween II* (1981)?
   a. Pepperoni
   b. Anchovies
   c. Sausage
   d. Mushrooms

2) What breakfast cereal is being eaten in the Myers house at the start of the 2007 *Halloween* remake?
   a. Lucky Charms
   b. Frosted Raisin Chunks
   c. Sugar Rice Pops
   d. Puffed Wheat

3) What type of cereal is John Tate eating for breakfast in *Halloween H20: 20 Years Later*?
   a. Frosted Flakes
   b. Life
   c. Maple-O's
   d. Frosted Sugar Bombs

4) What type of sandwich did Tommy Doyle want in the 2007 *Halloween* remake?
   a. Jelly and cream cheese sandwich
   b. Fried bologna sandwich
   c. Pork roll, egg, and cheese sandwich
   d. Jelly sandwich

5) What is Michael drinking when we see the first recorded session between Dr. Loomis and himself in the 2007 *Halloween* remake?
   a. Milk
   b. Orange juice
   c. Pepsi
   d. Barq's root beer

6) Sheriff Brackett opts for what breakfast food instead of Annie's scrambled egg whites in *Halloween II* (2009)?
   a. Krispy Kreme glazed doughnut
   b. Sticky buns
   c. Jelly doughnut
   d. Egg McMuffin

Halloween II replica mask from a photo where Dick Warlock was holding a can of Coke while wearing the mask. (*Photo courtesy: handiboy.com*)

"Hey jerk! Speed kills!"
— Annie Brackett (Halloween (1978))

MOTORIN'

Answers on page 288

Match these automobiles to their owners/drivers.

1) 1949 Dodge ½ Ton Pickup

2) 1975 Winnebago Indian

3) 1998 GMC Jimmy SLT

4) 1975 Ford Econoline Van

5) 1982 Oldsmobile Cutlass Supreme

6) 1987 Volkswagon Golf II

7) 1971 Cadillac Fleetwood 75

    a. Ellie Grimbridge   e. Buddy Kupfer

    b. Keri Tate   f. Bob Simms

    c. Becks   g. Rev. Jackson P. Sayer

    d. Conal Cochran

RIDE ON
Answers on page 289

Questions all about some automobiles in the films.

1) What type of car was Dr. Loomis driving before it was blown up at the gas station in *Halloween 4: The Return of Michael Myers?*
   a. Chevy Malibu
   b. Ford Escort
   c. Dodge Omni
   d. Oldsmobile Calais

2) What does Sara use to get around campus in *Halloween: Resurrection?*
   a. Golf cart
   b. Segway scooter
   c. Motorized wheelchair
   d. Yamaha Riva scooter

3) What did Wolfie name his van in *Halloween II* (2009)?
   a. The Wolfmobile
   b. The Howling
   c. The Mystery Machine
   d. The Shaggin' Wagon

4) What type of truck does Jamie use to escape to the bus depot in *Halloween: The Curse of Michael Myers?*
   a. Dodge Ram
   b. Toyota Tundra
   c. GMC Sierra
   d. Chevy Silverado

5) What type of car did Harry Grimbridge drive, which was spotted by his daughter Ellie in the Silver Shamrock factory in *Halloween III: Season of the Witch*?
   a. Blue panel van
   b. Red pickup truck
   c. Green station wagon
   d. Brown El Camino

6) Dr. Loomis and Nurse Marion Chambers are driving in what type of car, which is stolen by Michael Myers, in the original *Halloween* (1978)?
   a. 1977 Pontiac Firebird
   b. 1976 Ford LTD Station Wagon
   c. 1975 Ford Gran Torino
   d. 1969 Dodge Charger

7) What type of car does Norma drive *in Halloween H20: 20 Years Later*?
   a. 1957 Pontiac Bonneville
   b. 1958 Toyota Corona
   c. 1957 Ford Fairlane 500 Town Sedan
   d. 1958 Ford LTD Station Wagon

8) What kind of car does Laurie Strode drive in *Halloween II* (2009)?
   a. White Mitsubishi 3000GT
   b. Beige Honda Accord
   c. Blue Mazda RX7
   d. Red Toyota Prius

9) What type of car did Mikey own, which was taken by Michael Myers in *Halloween 5: The Revenge of Michael Myers?*
   a. 1966 Ford Mustang
   b. 1967 Chevy Camaro
   c. 1968 Chevy Corvette
   d. 1969 Dodge Charger

10) The Phelps Garage truck used in *Halloween* (1978) was borrowed from where?
   a. Donald Pleasence owned it
   b. John Carpenter's local mechanic
   c. Film's craft services company
   d. Debra Hill's father

11) What did the personalized license plate on Reverend Jackson P. Sayer's truck say in *Halloween 4: The Return of Michael Myers?*
   a. HOLY ROLLER
   b. REPENT
   c. AMEN
   d. JESUS SAVES

12) While most of the main vehicles in *Halloween* (1978) were carefully outfitted with Illinois license plates, what is the only vehicle seen with a California license plate?
   a. Annie's Chevy Monte Carlo
   b. Dr. Loomis's Ford LTD station wagon
   c. Lynda's Ford Pinto
   d. Bob's Ford Econoline van

THE OTHER SIDE
Answers on page 290

Questions all about *Halloween* franchise cast members in other things they have done.

1) Brad Dourif (Sheriff Brackett, Remakes) provided the voice for what other horror movie franchise's killer?

2) Al Berry (Harry Grimbridge, Part 3) portrayed Dr. Gruber in what Jeffrey Combs horror film?

3) Paul Rudd's (Tommy Doyle, Part 6) character Mike Hannigan dated which of the main characters on the TV show *Friends*?

4) Katee Sackhoff's (Jen, Part 8) best-known role is probably as Kara Thrace on a hit TV show; what is the better-known nickname of Kara Thrace?

5) Beau Starr (Sheriff Ben Meeker, Part 4) portrayed Henry Hill's father in what 1990 film?

6) Josh Hartnett (John Tate, *H20*) portrays American gunslinger Ethan Chandler, who teams up with an explorer and a medium to fight the supernatural in Victorian London in what Showtime original horror series?

7) Troy Evans (Deputy Charlie Bloch, *Halloween 5*) portrayed front desk clerk and former police officer Frank Martin for nine seasons on what TV medical drama?

8) Howard Hesseman (Uncle Meat, Remake 2) portrayed The Chief in what film that had multiple endings?

9) Bill Moseley's (Z-Man, Remake) first big role was as Chop-Top Sawyer in which installment of *The Texas Chainsaw Massacre* movie franchise?

10) Danny Trejo (Ismael Cruz, Remake) has portrayed the character Razor Charlie in all three films of what horror movie franchise and is the only person to appear in all three films?

11) Adam Arkin (Will Brennan, *H20*) starred as Dr. Aaron Shutt in what medical drama while filming *Halloween H20: 20 Years Later*?

12) Scout Taylor-Compton (Laurie Strode, Remakes) starred as Torrance Caldwell in what other remake of a 1986 horror film (which wasn't much of a remake as they changed most of the story)?

13) Margot Kidder (Barbara Collier, Remake 2) starred as Kathy Lutz alongside James Brolin in what 1979 horror film?

14) Lance Guest (Jimmy, Part 2) went on to appear in which *Jaws* film?

15) Which *Halloween* franchise cast member was the first African-American to appear on the covers of the Sports Illustrated Swimsuit Edition, GQ, and the Victoria's Secret catalog?

16) Dee Wallace (Cynthia Strode, Remake) portrayed Donna Trenton in what horror film based on a Stephen King novel?

17) Ken Foree (Big Joe Grizzly, Remake) said the same line, "When there's no more room in hell, the dead will walk the Earth," as different characters in what 1978 horror film and its 2004 remake?

18) Weird Al Yankovic (himself, Remake 2) starred as George Newman, who became station manager of struggling Channel 62, in what 1989 film that was shot mainly in Tulsa, Oklahoma?

19) Sasha Jenson (Brady, Part 4) portrayed Grueller in what 1992 Joss Whedon film, which led to a long-running TV series with a cult following and a spin-off?

20) Kyle Richards (Lindsey Wallace, Part 1) is a cast member of *The Real Housewives* of which city?
a. Atlanta   c. New Jersey
b. Beverly Hills   d. New York

21) Sid Haig (Chester Chesterfield, Remake) portrayed the Royal Apothecary of which villain in the 1960s Batman TV series?
a. Louie the Lilac   c. King Tut
b. Egghead   d. Colonel Gumm

22) Micky Dolenz (Derek Allen, Remake) provided the voice of what TV cartoon superhero's sidekick in the mid-1990s?
a. Freakazoid!   c. Space Ghost
b. The Tick   d. Batman

23) Michael Pataki (Dr. Hoffman, Part 4) was the first person to speak what language on the original Star Trek series in a memorable 1967 episode?
a. Vulcan   c. Klingon
b. Romulan   d. Andorian

24) Daniel Roebuck (Big Lou Martini, Remakes) starred as what real-life character in the TV movie *The Late Shift*?
a. David Letterman   c. Jay Leno
b. Tom Snyder   d. Johnny Carson

25) Dee Wallace (Cynthia Strode, Remake) will be
    appearing in what film that is co-written by *Friday
    the 13ᵗʰ* (1980) writer/creator Victor Miller and
    stars many other horror icons as well?
    a. *Simon Says Die*   c. *Hide and Go Kill*
    b. *Rock Paper Dead*   d. *Duck, Duck, Noose*

26) Richard Riehle (Buddy the Night Watchman,
    Remake 2) starred as Principal Ed Rooney in the
    TV version of what John Hughes film?
    a. *Pretty in Pink*
    b. *Weird Science*
    c. *The Breakfast Club*
    d. *Ferris Bueller's Day Off*

27) Nick Mennel (Bob Simms, Remake) also
    portrayed Mike in what other horror movie
    reboot?
    a. *A Nightmare on Elm Street*
    b. *The Texas Chainsaw Massacre*
    c. *Evil Dead*
    d. *Friday the 13ᵗʰ*

28) Jonathan Terry (Starker, Part 3) portrayed
    Colonel Glover in what other horror movie
    franchise?
    a. *Return of the Living Dead*
    b. *Hellraiser*
    c. *Phantasm*
    d. *Saw*

29) Kim Darby (Debra Strode, Part 6) was John Wayne's leading lady in which of his classic westerns?
   a. *True Grit*
   b. *McLintock!*
   c. *Rio Bravo*
   d. *The Sons of Katie Elder*

30) Actress Pamela Susan Shoop (Karen, Part 2) co-starred alongside Joan Collins, who was a scam artist trying to sell phony real estate in the Florida Everglades, in what 1977 horror film based on an H.G. Wells story about insects that are transformed into giants?
   a. *Food of the Gods*
   b. *The Shape of Things to Come*
   c. *Empire of the Ants*
   d. *Village of the Giants*

31) Mitchell Ryan (Dr. Wynn, Part 6) portrayed the estranged father of which of the Enterprise's crew in an episode of *Star Trek: The Next Generation*?
   a. Chief Miles O'Brien
   b. Doctor Beverly Crusher
   c. Commander William Riker
   d. Counselor Deanna Troi

32) LL Cool J (Ronny, *H20*) made his film debut
   when he was just 17 years old, portraying himself
   as a budding rap star in what 1985 film that
   starred many rap greats of the time?
   a. *Krush Groove*
   b. *Wild Style*
   c. *Beat Street*
   d. *Breakin' 2: Electric Boogaloo*

33) What actress from the *Halloween* movie franchise
   is co-founder and hostess of the Hot Springs
   Horror Film Festival, which has been held yearly
   since 2013 in her hometown of Hot Springs,
   Arkansas?
   a. Wendy Kaplan   c. Danielle Harris
   b. Tamara Glynn   d. Katee Sackhoff

34) Actor Billy Warlock (Craig, Part 2) portrayed
   which member of the Brady family on the day-
   time soap opera *Days of Our Lives*?
   a. Sami Brady   c. Frankie Brady
   b. Peter Brady   d. Oliver Brady

35) Howard Hesseman (Uncle Meat, Remake 2) had
   a recurring role in all but which one of these TV
   shows?
   a. *WKRP in Cincinnati*   c. *Head of the Class*
   b. *The Golden Palace*   d. *One Day at a Time*

36) Chris Hardwick (David Newman, Remake 2) got his big break as co-host of what MTV show alongside Jenny McCarthy?
   a. *Shipmates*
   b. *Remote Control*
   c. *Headbanger's Ball*
   d. *Singled Out*

37) Actress Ana Alicia (Janet, *Halloween II*) portrayed both Melissa Agretti and Samantha Ross on what nighttime serial drama?
   a. *Falcon Crest*
   b. *Knots Landing*
   c. *Dallas*
   d. *Dynasty*

38) Kathleen Kinmont (Kelly Meeker, Part 4) portrayed Gloria in what other 1980s horror movie sequel?
   a. *Ghoulies II*
   b. *Fright Night II*
   c. *Slumber Party Massacre 2*
   d. *Bride of Re-Animator*

39) Lisa Gay Hamilton (Shirl, *H20*) portrayed Rebecca Washington on what popular law drama?
   a. *Boston Legal*
   b. *L.A. Law*
   c. *The Practice*
   d. *Law & Order: Trial by Jury*

40) Stacey Nelkin (Ellie Grimbridge, Part 3) was the inspiration for Mariel Hemmingway's character Tracy in which Woody Allen film after he dated her while she was a teenager?
   a. *Manhattan*
   b. *Annie Hall*
   c. *Stardust Memories*
   d. *Hannah and Her Sisters*

41) Matthew Walker (Spitz, Part 5) portrayed Ellis in Part 3 of which other horror movie franchise?
   a. *A Nightmare on Elm Street*
   b. *The Texas Chainsaw Massacre*
   c. *Scream*
   d. *Child's Play*

42) Brad Dourif (Sheriff Brackett, Remakes) also portrayed The Gemini Killer in the third installment of what other horror franchise in 1990?
   a. *Underworld*
   b. *Puppet Master*
   c. *The Exorcist*
   d. *Witchboard*

43) Mary Birdsong (Nancy McDonald, Remake 2) starred as rookie Deputy Cherisa Kimball in what comedy series?
   a. *Brooklyn Nine-Nine*   c. *Reno 911!*
   b. *My Name Is Earl*   d. *Psych*

44) Sean Patrick Thomas (Rudy, Part 8) portrayed Detective Temple Page in what crime drama set in Washington, D.C. and starring Craig T. Nelson?
   a. *The Agency*   c. *J.A.G.*
   b. *The District*   d. *N.C.I.S.*

45) Octavia Spencer (Nurse Octavia Daniels, Remake 2) won an Academy Award for her role in which film?
   a. *The Help*   c. *Bad Santa*
   b. *Black or White*   d. *Paradise*

46) Sheri Moon Zombie (Deborah Myers, Remakes) portrayed Daisy Rain in what 2004 Tobe Hooper-directed film, one of the few things she has been in that Rob Zombie was not involved in?
   a. *Art of the Devil* c. *Crocodile*
   b. *Toolbox Murders*   d. *Dracula 3000*

47) Gene Ross (Earl, Part 4) also had a small role as an unnamed police officer directing traffic at a crime scene at the start of Part 4 of what other horror movie franchise?
   a. *House*   c. *Friday the 13th*
   b. *A Nightmare on Elm* d. *Silent Night, Deadly*
      Street   *Night*

48) Dan O'Herlihy (Conal Cochran, Part 3) was nominated for a 1955 Academy Award for his starring role in what film?

   a. *Robinson Crusoe*   c. *The Caine Mutiny*

   b. *On the Waterfront*   d. *Rear Window*

49) Caroline Williams (Dr. Maple, Remake Part 2) portrayed Vanita "Stretch" Brock in which horror movie sequel?

   a. *Phantasm IV: Oblivion*

   b. *A Nightmare on Elm Street 5: The Dream Child*

   c. *Hellraiser: Bloodline*

   d. *The Texas Chainsaw Massacre 2*

Halloween: Resurrection – Merry Clown mask worn by Harold the serial killer fanatic inmate at Grace Anderson Sanitarium.
(Photo courtesy: Kevin S. King)

ALWAYS SOMETHING THERE TO REMIND ME
Answers on page 293

Questions all about some things that were reused/redone in later films of the franchise.

1) In *Halloween H20: Twenty Years Later,* Keri/Laurie's assistant Norma says, "Everyone is entitled to one good scare." This line was first said by what character in the original *Halloween* (1978)?

2) What last name was shared by a doctor and then a professor at Haddonfield University in a later film in the *Halloween* movie franchise?

3) What type of doll did Laurie Strode have on her dresser in the original *Halloween* (1978), a doll which makes another appearance in *H20* where Laurie uses it to hide her medicine?

4) The Rabbit in Red Lounge being used as Deborah Myers's work place is an homage to the original film, where which character introduced it into the *Halloween* film universe?

5) Lynda's boyfriend Bob Simms puts on which costume (complete with his own glasses) in the 2007 remake, a callback to what Michael dressed as to disguise himself from her in the original film?

THE NIGHT OF THE WARLOCK
Answers on page 293

Questions all about Dick Warlock.

1) Dick Warlock was the stunt coordinator on which of the *Friday the 13th* sequels?
   a. *Friday the 13th Part 3*
   b. *Friday the 13th: The Final Chapter*
   c. *Friday the 13th: A New Beginning*
   d. *Jason Lives: Friday the 13th Part VI*

2) Dick Warlock was the stunt double for which actor in *Jaws*?
   a. Roy Scheider   c. Carl Gottlieb
   b. Robert Shaw   d. Richard Dreyfuss

3) Dick Warlock was the stunt coordinator for the second and third installments of which horror movie franchise?
   a. *Child's Play*
   b. *Tremors*
   c. *Silent Night, Deadly Night*
   d. *A Nightmare On Elm Street*

4) Dick Warlock was a regular stunt double for which actor on more than 30 projects, including films like *Unlawful Entry* and *The Best of Times*?
   a. Ray Liotta   c. Kurt Russell
   b. Robin Williams   d. Donald Moffat

AMONG THE LIVING

A list of all the main survivors from the films.

Film	Main Survivors	Notes
Halloween (1978)	Laurie Strode, Dr. Loomis, Sheriff Brackett, Dr. Terrence Wynn, Marion Chambers, Tommy Doyle, Lindsey Wallace	All but Lindsey returned for at least one more film in the franchise. There was a character named Lindsey that was supposed to be her in *Halloween 4*. They decided to not expand the storyline in the end, so she was just a random friend that drove Rachel and Jamie to the store.
Halloween II (1981)	Laurie Strode, Dr. Loomis, Sheriff Brackett, Marion Chambers, Jimmy	All but Sheriff Brackett and Jimmy return for another film. Jimmy's survival is in question in the theatrical release, but in the TV version he is seen alive and well in the end.
Halloween III: Season of the Witch	Dr. Daniel Challis	Dr. Challis is the only main character that can definitively be identified as a survivor.

Halloween 4: The Return of Michael Myers	Jamie Lloyd, Dr. Loomis, Rachel Carruthers, Sheriff Ben Meeker, Richard Carruthers Darlene Carruthers	Other than Richard Carruthers, they would all return for Part 5. Darlene Carruthers was just in voice though.
Halloween 5: The Revenge of Michael Myers	Jamie Lloyd, Dr. Loomis, The Man in Black (Dr. Wynn)	All would return for Part 6.
Halloween: The Curse of Michael Myers	Dr. Loomis, Tommy Doyle, Kara Strode, Steven Lloyd	None of them would be heard from again.
Halloween H20: Twenty Years Later	Laurie Strode, Molly, John Tate, Ronny, Norma	Only Laurie would return for *Resurrection.*
Halloween: Resurrection	Sara Moyer, Freddie Harris, Myles Barton	It is doubtful any of them would have returned if the franchise had another sequel.
Halloween (2007)	Laurie Strode Annie Brackett, Dr. Loomis, Sheriff Lee Brackett, Tommy Doyle, Lindsey Wallace	Laurie, Annie, Dr. Loomis, and Sheriff Brackett all returned for Part 2.
Halloween II (2009)	Sheriff Lee Brackett	In the end we see Laurie, Dr. Loomis, and even Michael all presumably die.

"Michael's work is not finished in Haddonfield. And soon, very soon, he'll come back."
— Tommy Doyle (Halloween: The Curse of Michael Myers)

INDESTRUCTIBLE

A list of how people tried to kill Michael Myers in the films.

Halloween **(1978)**	Dr. Loomis shoots him six times, sending him off a second story balcony. He disappears minutes later when they check on him.
Halloween II **(1981)**	Dr. Loomis and Laurie fill the hospital room with ether and oxygen. Loomis shoots Michael again and then blows them both up. Michael appears to die a fiery death.
Halloween 4: The Return of Michael Myers	Rachel Carruthers hits Michael with a truck, sending him down a hill. Michael wanders off into a drainage sewer.
Halloween 5: The Revenge of Michael Myers	Was not killed, but instead locked in a cell.
Halloween: The Curse of Michael Myers	Left for dead in Smith's Grove Sanitarium. Dr. Loomis stays there, but we do not see what ultimately happens. In the producer's cut, Michael switches clothes with Dr.

	Wynn and walks away.
Halloween H20: Twenty Years Later	Laurie decapitates Michael with an axe. However, we later learn that he switched clothes again and got away.
Halloween: Resurrection	Freddie Harris electrocutes Michael after a fight. He later opens his eyes in the morgue.
Halloween (2007)	The last thing we see is Laurie and Michael struggling when her gun goes off, pointed in the general direction of his head.
Halloween II (2009)	A barrage of bullets from many sheriffs take Michael down after he stabs Dr. Loomis.

THE NUMBERS OF THE BEAST
Answers on page 293

1) What was Dr. Hoffman's telephone number in *Halloween 4: The Return of Michael Myers?*
   a. (555) 555-1234   c. (123) 456-7890
   b. (311) 555-2368   d. (867) 530-9999

2) What do the letters of the 1-800 telephone number for the call-in radio show Back Talk spell out?
   a. Talk 2 Me   c. You Suck
   b. Bak Talk   d. O Bite Me

3) What is the room number in which Freddie Harris is staying in *Halloween: Resurrection?*
   a. 274   c. 1031
   b. 666   d. 1313

4) What is the telephone number for the Rose of Shannon Motel in *Halloween III: Season of the Witch?*
   a. 555-ROSE (7673)   c. 555-3795
   b. 555-1111   d. 555-2462

5) The hydrotherapy pool at Haddonfield Memorial Hospital should not exceed what temperature, according to a safety sign near its controls in *Halloween II* (1981)?
   a. 90 degrees   c. 110 degrees
   b. 100 degrees   d. 120 degrees

6) What number is given to the Michael Myers case?
   a. #103178   c. #11425
   b. #666666   d. #54321

7) What room do Daniel and Ellie stay in at the
   motel in *Halloween III: Season of the Witch?*
   a. Room 5   c. Room 7
   b. Room 6   d. Room 8

8) How long did the State Police tell Rachel it would
   take them to get to Haddonfield in *Halloween 4:
   The Return of Michael Myers?*
   a. 15 minutes   c. 35 minutes
   b. 25 minutes   d. 45 minutes

9) What was Laurie Strode's room number at Grace
   Anderson Sanitarium in *Halloween: Resurrection?*
   a. 6-L   c. 5-R
   b. 13-F   d. 1031

10) How many times has Jimmy been suspended,
   "for getting a little crazy with the stick," in
   Halloween H20: 20 Years Later?
   a. 5   c. 7
   b. 6   d. 8

11) What number is on Tony's hockey jersey in
   Halloween H20: 20 Years Later?
   a. 20   c. 17
   b. 78   d. 00

HEAVEN AND HELL

Laurie Strode has an opening narration in *Halloween: Resurrection*. She says it as we enter the door to her then home, the Grace Anderson Sanitarium – Psychiatric Care Facility, and see some of the inmates.

"You've heard of the tunnel. The one we all go through sooner or later. At the end there's a door, and waiting for you on the other side of that door is either Heaven or Hell. This is that door."

"Never underestimate the effect of a poor diet. Too much protein, not enough zinc. Next thing you know, you're cutting up bodies in the bathtub. I mean, look at Hitler. He was a vegetarian. The brother was seriously malnourished."
    – *Rudy Grimes (Halloween: Resurrection)*

NONSTOP TO NOWHERE
Answers on page 294

Questions all about some random people and things in the films.

1) What is the name of the woman that gets Dr. Mixter his coffee and ultimately finds him dead in his office in *Halloween II* (1981)?
   a. Virginia Alves
   b. Karen Rainey
   c. Janet Newhall
   d. Jill Wells

2) Which of the girls was suspended from the cheerleading squad in the 2007 *Halloween* remake?
   a. Laurie
   b. Annie
   c. Lynda
   d. Lindsey

3) What sport were Jimmy and Tony participating in when we first see them in *Halloween H20: 20 Years Later*?
   a. Baseball   c. Basketball
   b. Football   d. Hockey

4) What toy can be seen in front of the TV as Michael Myers enters the house to go kill his sister in the original *Halloween* (1978)?
   a. Tonka dump truck
   b. Firetruck
   c. Barbie Dream Car
   d. Remote control helicopter

5) Upon its release, *Halloween II* (1981) was banned in which two countries due to graphic violence and nudity?
   a. Romania and Poland
   b. Australia and Monaco
   c. Iceland and West Germany
   d. Bolivia and New Zealand

6) What does Tommy Doyle tell Laurie about when they meet up while walking to school on Halloween morning in the 2007 *Halloween* remake?
   a. A Mexican wolfman named Danny
   b. Aliens landing in Roswell, NM
   c. The Donner Party Incident
   d. The Manson Family Murders

7) What type of pin does Nurse Jill Franco have on her collar in *Halloween II* (1981)?
   a. A clown mask
   b. A ghost
   c. A spider web
   d. A pumpkin with a black cat in it

8) The original *Halloween* (1978) was nominated in 1979 by the Academy of Science Fiction, Fantasy & Horror Films for a Saturn Award for Best Horror Film; to what 1973 film did it lose out?
   a. *The Exorcist*
   b. *The Wicker Man*
   c. *The Texas Chainsaw Massacre*
   d. *Jaws*

9) Richard Delmer Boyer was convicted and sentenced to death for killing elderly couple Francis and Eileen Harbitz in El Monte, California after he claimed to have hallucinations that he was re-enacting which *Halloween* film?
   a. *Halloween II* (1981)
   b. *Halloween 4: The Return of Michael Myers*
   c. *Halloween: The Curse of Michael Myers*
   d. *Halloween* (1978)

10) What weapon does Sara use against Michael Myers while in the control room in *Halloween: Resurrection*?
   a. Machete
   b. Butcher Knife
   c. Chainsaw
   d. Freddy Krueger glove she took from a costumed child

11) What was the name of the martial artist that Freddie Harris is obsessed with and watching on TV in his hotel room in *Halloween: Resurrection*?
   a. Wat Chun Lee   c. Bolo Yeung
   b. Bruce Lee   d. Gordon Liu

12) In *Halloween 4: The Return of Michael Myers*, we learn from Deputy Pierce that Sheriff Brackett has retired to which Florida city?
   a. Orlando   c. Miami
   b. St. Petersburg   d. Pensacola

13) What card game do the two deputies play in the car while sitting outside the Tower Farm Party to protect Tina in *Halloween 5: The Revenge of Michael Myers*?
   a. Crazy 8's   c. Poker
   b. Go Fish   d. Pinochle

14) What did Michael Myers use to bar the back door at the Wallace house so Laurie couldn't escape in the original *Halloween* (1978)?
   a. Tree branch   c. Patio chair
   b. Fence post   d. Rake

15) Which actress reportedly got an ear infection after shooting her death scene due to the water used for the scene being dirty?
   a. Tyra Banks   c. Pamela Susan Shoop
   b. J.C. Brandy   d. Tamara Glynn

16) John Strode says that his daughter Kara
   disappeared for how many years in *Halloween: The
   Curse of Michael Myers?*
   a. 3 Years
   b. 4 Years
   c. 5 Years
   d. 6 Years

17) What is the name of the judge that presided over
   Michael Myers's case in the 2007 *Halloween*
   remake?
   a. Judge Sheindlin
   b. Judge Masterson
   c. Judge Wilbur
   d. Judge Ito

18) A caller to the Back Talk radio show had the
   theory that what law enforcement agency
   abducted Michael Myers in *Halloween 6: The Curse
   of Michael Myers?*
   a. F.B.I.
   b. N.C.I.S.
   c. C.I.A.
   d. D.E.A.

19) Sheriff Meeker says that who will be coming to
   take Michael Myers to a maximum security
   facility at the end of *Halloween 5: The Revenge of
   Michael Myers?*
   a. State Police   c. F.B.I.
   b. National Guard   d. N.S.A.

20) What unusual item can clearly be seen mixed in with all the tools in the store room at Haddonfield Memorial Hospital in *Halloween II* (1981)?
   a. Hockey mask
   b. Bedpan
   c. Meat thermometer
   d. Prosthetic leg

21) What does Michael do with the knife that he stabbed Laurie with right before she fell to her death in *Halloween: Resurrection*?
   a. Gave it to an inmate of the sanitarium
   b. Dropped down onto her dead body
   c. Stuck it in the door to the roof
   d. Stuck it in a picture of Laurie's son John

22) What gift does Deborah Myers give young Michael while at Smith's Grove Sanitarium at the start of *Halloween II* (2009)?
   a. Clown mask
   b. Book of Edgar Allan Poe stories
   c. White horse statue
   d. Papier mache kit

23) Where does Michael Myers leave Mrs. Elrod's knife while he is in the elementary school?
   a. Stuck in the blackboard
   b. Stuck in a classroom door
   c. Stuck in the sister of a family drawing
   d. Stuck in a custodian

24) Why was Susan Pierce not able to babysit Jamie Lloyd on Halloween in *Halloween 4: The Return of Michael Myers?*
   a. She broke her ankle at the ice skating rink
   b. She had to have an emergency appendectomy
   c. She broke her arm playing field hockey
   d. She got into a car accident

25) Dr. Loomis and Laurie Strode begin turning on tanks that contained what two items near the end of *Halloween II* (1981)?
   a. Hydrogen and oxygen
   b. Nitrous oxide and ether
   c. Ether and oxygen
   d. Propane and natural gas

Halloween (2007) jack-o-lantern put over Paul's head after his murder

WE ARE FAMILY

Throughout the movies, there have been quite a few familial relationships. Here is a list of them all.

(Note: All Michael Myers relatives are listed in "The Roots of All Evil" table on page .)

Characters	Relationship	Notes
Sheriff Leigh/Lee and Annie Brackett	Father and daughter	Both characters appeared in the original and remakes *Halloween* and *Halloween II*, although Annie was a corpse in the original sequel. Sheriff Brackett's first name spelling was changed for the remakes.
Morgan and Laurie Strode	Father and adopted daughter	Laurie's mother is not named in the films until the remake.
Unnamed parents and Lindsey Wallace	Father, mother, and daughter	Lindsey's parents are seen in the original but not named.
Mr. and Mrs. Elrod	Husband and wife	Michael Myers sneaks into their house to steal a knife in *Halloween II*
Unnamed mother and Gary	Mother and son	They are seen going to the hospital after Gary bit into a razor blade in *Halloween II*
Dr. Daniel, Linda, Bella, and Willie Challis	Father, mother, daughter, and son	Daniel and Linda are divorced.

Harry and Ellie Grimbridge	Father and daughter	Ellie, with the help of Dr. Challis, investigates her father's murder in *Halloween III: Season of the Witch*.
Buddy, Betty, and Little Buddy Kupfer	Father, mother, son	The family get a special tour of the Silver Shamrock Novelties factory for being #1 in sales for the year; it doesn't end well for them though.
Richard, Darlene, and Rachel Carruthers	Father, mother, and daughter	The Carruthers family take in Jamie Lloyd as a foster child after her parents were killed.
Sheriff Ben and Kelly Meeker	Father and daughter	Another single father sheriff. What are the odds?
Deputy and Susan Pierce	Father and daughter	Susan is the Carruthers' babysitter that cancels over the phone.
Laurie Strode and Jamie and Steven Lloyd	Mother, daughter, and grandson/son	Both Jamie's and Steven's fathers are not definitively named.
John, Debra, Kara, Tim, and Danny Strode	Father, mother, daughter, son, and Kara's son	John was Morgan Strode's brother, making him Laurie's adopted uncle.
Claudia and Casey	Mother and daughter	Two random characters which Michael came across in a rest stop and took their car.

Keri and John Tate	Mother and son	Keri is of course Laurie Strode living under a fake name after faking her death.
Mason, Cynthia, and Laurie Strode	Father, mother, and daughter	These were Laurie's adoptive parents in the remake. Neither made it to Part Two.
Noel Kluggs and Jack Kendall	Cousins	Both worked as guards at Smith's Grove.
Floyd, Sherman and Jazlean Benny	Relationship unsure. Floyd is Jazlean's father. Sherman could be either her brother or her husband.	Family in the truck that beat Michael for being on their land in *Halloween II* remake.
Kyle and Lynda Van Der Klok	Father and daughter	Lynda was killed in the previous film, but her father confronted Dr. Loomis in the *Halloween II* remake.

"Freaks will always find their way home."
– Dr. Loomis, by way of his Aunt Vera (Halloween II (2009))

ALL IN THE FAMILY

Answers on page 295

Questions all about some real-life famous relatives of the *Halloween* franchise cast members.

1) Which Michael Myers actor's father choreographed dance scenes in classic films like *Royal Wedding, The Little Princess,* and *Buck Privates?*
   a. Dick Warlock
   b. Tyler Mane
   c. Nick Castle
   d. Tommy Lee Wallace

2) Which *Halloween 4: The Return of Michael Myers* cast member's mother, Abby Dalton, once portrayed her future real-life son-in-law's (Lorenzo Llamas) mother on the show *Falcon Crest?*
   a. Ellie Cornell
   b. Kathleen Kinmont
   c. Danielle Harris
   d. Karen Alston

3) Joshua John Miller (William Challis, Part 3) is the half-brother of which *Lost Boys* cast member?
   a. Corey Feldman
   b. Kiefer Sutherland
   c. Corey Haim
   d. Jason Patric

4) Which *Halloween* franchise actress's father flew the first photographic reconnaissance mission over Omaha Beach on D-Day and would later become vice president of the Howard Hughes Aircraft Company?
   a. Jamie Lee Curtis
   b. P.J. Soles
   c. Gloria Gifford
   d. Pamela Susan Shoop

5) Sasha Jenson's (Brady, Part 4) father Roy portrayed a thug that got to rough up Jack Nicholson's character J.J. Gittes a bit in what 1974 film?
   a. *Chinatown*
   b. *Carnal Knowledge*
   c. *The King of Marvin Gardens*
   d. *One Flew Over the Cuckoo's Nest*

WORD UP

Answers on page 296

Questions all about some things that we see written in places in the films.

1) What does Jim say it said on the arm that fell on him, which led him to realize it was fake and all set up by Freddie, in *Halloween: Resurrection?*
   a. Recyclable
   b. Made in Taiwan
   c. Made in China
   d. Made in the U.S.A.

2) Which phrase can be seen written on Ronnie's arm cast in the 2007 *Halloween* remake?
   a. SUCK IT
   b. BITE ME
   c. FREDDY RULEZ!
   d. BEARS RULE!

3) What does Michael Myers write on the inside of the door of his cell/room at Smith's Grove Sanitarium before he breaks out, as can be seen in the added TV scenes of the original *Halloween* (1978)?
   a. LAURIE
   b. SISTER
   c. CYNTHIA
   d. BOO

4) What did the note that was attached to a rock and thrown through Jamie's window in *Halloween 5: The Revenge of Michael Myers* say?
   a. She is the Devil!
   b. The evil child must die!
   c. The child is cursed!
   d. Michael will get you!

5) What did Jamie Lloyd write on the small blackboard while sitting in bed at the start of *Halloween 5: The Revenge of Michael Myers*?
   a. Uncle Michael is coming home again.
   b. Help Me!
   c. The Boogeyman is coming!
   d. He is coming for me.

TURN THE PAGE

A comprehensive list of all the novelizations of the films and other novels based on the story of Halloween.

Novelizations		
Title	**Author**	**Publisher, Date**
Halloween	Curtis Richards (Dennis Etchison)	Bantam Books, 1979
Halloween II	Jack Martin (Dennis Etchison)	Zabra, November 1, 1981
Halloween III	Jack Martin (Dennis Etchison)	Jove, October 1, 1984
Halloween IV	Nicholas Grabowsky	Lorevan Publishing October, 1988 Re-released – BookSurge Publishing, September 25, 2003
Novels Based Upon *Halloween* and Michael Myers		
The Scream Factory	Kelly O'Rourke	Berkley, October 1, 1997
A group of friends sets up a haunted house in the basement of Haddonfield City Hall. Michael Myers systematically kills them all.		
The Old Myers Place	Kelly O'Rourke	Berkley, December 1, 1997
Mary White's family moves to Haddonfield, and more importantly into the Myers house. Now that she is starting to fit in her new home, she will have to fight off Michael Myers, who decides to return home.		
The Mad House	Kelly O'Rourke	Berkley, February 1, 1998
Christine Ray is bored with summer until she sees an ad looking for a volunteer film crew to make a documentary about Smith's Grove. To do so, they must stay in the hospital overnight. They soon realize Michael is still inside its walls and ready to kill them all.		

"In England, I'm a horror movie director. In Germany, I'm a filmmaker. In the U.S., I'm a bum."
— John Carpenter

DIRECTOR'S SLASH

Answers on page 296

Questions all about other things done by the directors of the *Halloween* films.

1) Who is the only director other than Rob Zombie to direct more than one *Halloween* film?

2) Director Rob Zombie went on to make what Halloween- (the holiday, not the film) related horror movie with Malcolm McDowell starring as Father Murder?

3) *Halloween 5: The Revenge of Michael Myers* director Dominique Othenin-Girard also directed the fourth installment of what other horror movie franchise, which was subtitled *The Awakening*?

4) Which *Halloween* film director also directed horror icon Robert Englund in 1989's *Phantom of the Opera*?
   a. Nick Castle
   b. Dwight H. Little
   c. Tommy Lee Wallace
   d. Joe Chapelle

5) Which *Halloween H20: Twenty Years Later* co-star had an uncredited role in director Steve Miner's next film, *Lake Placid*?
   a. Jamie Lee Curtis
   b. Josh Hartnett
   c. Adam Arkin
   d. Michelle Williams

6) Director Rick Rosenthal also directed which TV sequel to an Alfred Hitchcock film under the alias Alan Smithee?
   a. *Rear Window 2*
   b. *Spellbound 2*
   c. *Vertigo 2: Another Obsession*
   d. *The Birds II: Land's End*

7) As well as writing/directing *Halloween III*, Tommy Lee Wallace also wrote which two 1980's horror movie sequels?
   a. *Amityville II: The Possession*
   b. *Poltergeist II: The Other Side*
   c. *Fright Night II*
   d. *Phantasm II*

8) What other Rick Rosenthal-directed film has a scene with a theater marquee showing that *Halloween II* is playing?
   a. *American Dreamer*
   b. *Bad Boys*
   c. *Distant Thunder*
   d. *Beverly Hills Cop II*

9) *Halloween 6* director Joe Chappelle would later direct fellow *Halloween* alum Brad Dourif in an episode of what Joshua Jackson TV series?
   a. *Dawson's Creek*
   b. *Supernatural*
   c. *The Affair*
   d. *Fringe*

10) Cast members of the *Halloween* remake staged a takeover of what CBS crime drama in an episode titled "L.A.," which was directed by Rob Zombie and featured Sheri Moon Zombie, Kristina Klebe, William Forsythe, and Malcolm McDowell?
   a. *C.S.I.*
   b. *N.C.I.S.*
   c. *C.S.I.: Miami*
   d. *C.S.I.: New York*

11) Rob Zombie worked as a production assistant on what children's show in the 1980s?
   a. Sesame Street
   b. The Electric Company
   c. The Great Space Coaster
   d. Pee-Wee's Playhouse

COULD'VE BEEN

A comprehensive list of actors who almost made it into the *Halloween* films.

Person	Role	Notes
Anne Lockhart	Laurie Strode	Anne is the daughter of June Lockhart from *Lassie* and *Lost in Space* (and a lot more) fame. She was John Carpenter's first choice for the role but was tied up with other roles.
Peter Cushing	Dr. Samuel Loomis	Was one of Carpenter's top two choices, along with Lee. They both turned it down because it didn't pay enough.
Christopher Lee	Dr. Samuel Loomis	Lee would later say not taking the role was the biggest mistake of his career.
Dennis Quaid	*Halloween* (1978)	He and P.J. Soles were dating. They tried to get him for the role of Soles's movie boyfriend Bob Simms, but he couldn't due to a scheduling conflict.
Melissa Joan Hart	Jamie Lloyd – *Halloween 4: The Return of Michael Myers*	Auditioned

Rebecca Shaeffer	Rachel Carruthers – *Halloween 4: The Return of Michael Myers*	Auditioned – Shot dead by a stalker just 9 months after the release of the film.
Peter Jackson	Director – *Halloween: The Curse of Michael Myers*	Asked to direct; declined.
Denise Richards	Beth – *Halloween: The Curse of Michael Myers*	Considered for the role, but declined.
Howard Stern	Barry Simms – *Halloween: The Curse of Michael Myers*	Offered the role of the shock jock.
Christopher Lee	Dr. Terrance Wynn – *Halloween: The Curse of Michael Myers*	Lee was writer Daniel Farrands's first choice for the role.
Fred Walton	Originally set to direct *Halloween: The Curse of Michael Myers* but dropped out.	Walton was the director of films like *When a Stranger Calls* and *April Fool's Day*
P.J. Soles	Norma – *Halloween H20: Twenty Years Later*	Offered the role. She didn't like the idea of portraying a different character in the series.
Emma Stone	Laurie Strode – *Halloween* (2007)	Auditioned
Danielle Panabaker	Laurie Strode – *Halloween* (2007)	Auditioned
John Carpenter	*Halloween II* (2009)	Offered a cameo role by Rob Zombie

ADULT EDUCATION

Answers on page 297

Questions all about things perceived to be more "adult" in nature.

1) What is the name of the strip club where Deborah Myers dances in the 2007 *Halloween* remake?

2) Where were Nurse Karen Rainey and Paramedic Budd going to have sex in *Halloween II*?

3) What magazine is Big Joe Grizzly looking at in the bathroom in the 2007 *Halloween* remake before Michael Myers decides to borrow his clothes?
   a. Hustler
   b. Cheri
   c. Swank
   d. Big 'Uns

4) What brand of cigarettes does Lynda smoke after having sex in the original *Halloween* (1978)?
   a. Virginia Slims
   b. Kool 100s
   c. Parliaments
   d. Vantage

5) Which actress from the *Halloween* franchise was Playboy's Playmate of the Month for June 1974?
   a. Sandy Johnson   c. Stacey Nelkin
   b. P.J. Soles   d. Pamela Susan Shoop

6) Ellie Cornell (Rachel Carruthers, Part 4) portrayed a police detective on what Cinemax original adult series that tells stories in the style of a film noir-esque anthology?
   a. *Red Shoe Diaries*
   b. *Femme Fatales*
   c. *Sin City Diaries*
   d. *Passion Cove*

7) What brand of cigarettes does Nurse Marion Chambers smoke in the original *Halloween* (1978)?
   a. Marlboro 100s
   b. Virginia Slims
   c. Parliaments
   d. Benson & Hedges

RELEASE ME

A list of the release dates for all the films.

Film	Release Date
Halloween (1978)	October 25, 1978
Halloween II (1981)	October 30, 1981
Halloween III: Season of the Witch	October 22, 1982
Halloween 4: The Return of Michael Myers	October 21, 1988
Halloween 5: The Revenge of Michael Myers	October 13, 1989
Halloween: The Curse of Michael Myers	September 29, 1995
Halloween H20: Twenty Years Later	August 5, 1998
Halloween: Resurrection	July 12, 2002
Halloween (2007)	August 31, 2007
Halloween II (2009)	August 28, 2009

THE FINAL CUT

A list of all the budget and box office numbers for all the films.

Film	Budget	Box Office
Halloween (1978)	$300,000	$47,000,000
Halloween II (1981)	$2,500,000	$25,533,818
Halloween III: Season of the Witch	$2,500,000	$14,400,000
Halloween 4: The Return of Michael Myers	$5,000,000	$17,768,757
Halloween 5: The Revenge of Michael Myers	$6,332,000	$11,642,254
Halloween: The Curse of Michael Myers	$7,308,529	$15,116,634
Halloween H20: Twenty Years Later	$17,000,000	$55,041,738
Halloween: Resurrection	$15,000,000	$30,354,442
Halloween (2007)	$15,000,000	$58,272,029
Halloween II (2009)	$15,000,000	$33,392,973

TIMELINE

Halloween (1978)

Halloween night, Thursday, October 31, 1963: Judith Myers is killed by her brother Michael.

Monday, October 30, 1978: Michael escapes Smith's Grove.

Tuesday, October 31, 1978: All of the murders happen.

Halloween II (1981)

Tuesday, October 31, 1978: The night picks up where part one left off. Now Laurie is in the hospital and Michael follows.

Wednesday, November 1, 1978: Most (if not all) of the events actually take place after midnight as the original film had progressed well into the night.

Halloween III: Season of the Witch

Saturday, October 23, 1982: Harry Grimbridge is killed.

Sunday, October 24th, 1982: Ellie arrives at the hospital.

Wednesday, October 27th, 1982: Dr. Challis visits the coroner's office.

Friday, October 29th, 1982: Ellie meets up with Dr. Challis at the bar. They plan their visit to Santa Mira. Marge is killed at the hotel.

Saturday, October 30, 1982: Kupfer factory tour. Dr. Challis goes back that night to break in and discovers the first evidence of robots. He is taken captive.

Halloween, Sunday, October 31, 1982: Cochran gives his explanation and runs his test on the Kupfers. The time for the giveaway is upon us.

Halloween 4: The Return of Michael Myers

Monday, October 30, 1988: Michael escapes while being transported back to Smith's Grove. We meet Jamie Lloyd.

Tuesday, October 31, 1988: School, costume shopping, and all of the killing takes place.

Halloween 5: The Revenge of Michael Myers

Tuesday, October 30, 1989: Michael awakens from a coma and kills the Mountain Man. Jamie has her first vision.

Wednesday, October 31, 1989: Rachel and Tina visit Jamie and bring Max. Halloween parties take place, as do all of the killings. Michael and Jamie are kidnapped in the end.

Halloween: The Curse of Michael Myers

Monday, October 30, 1995: Jamie Lloyd gives birth and escapes. Michael hunts her down.

Tuesday, October 31, 1995: We meet Kara Strode and family, the rally takes place, and the rest of the killing happens.

Halloween H20: 20 Years Later

Thursday, October 29, 1998: Langdon, IL scenes; Michael kills Jimmy, Tony, and Nurse Marion Chambers-Whetington, and then heads to California.

Friday, October 30, 1998: Langdon detectives investigate at Marion's; we visit Headmistress Keri Tate's office as the clock hits midnight.

Saturday, October 31, 1998: We meet Keri Tate and her son John and learn that she is really Laurie Strode. Michael arrives in Summer Glen. Laurie decapitates who she thinks is Michael but turns out to be a paramedic.

Halloween: Resurrection

Wednesday, October 31, 2001: We see Laurie Strode institutionalized. Michael finds her and they battle to her death.

Prior to October 30, 2002: We meet Sara and friends and find out they will be part of the Dangertainment reality show.

Wednesday, October 30, 2002: Dangertainment orientation/publicity meeting

Thursday, October 31, 2002: Enter the Myers house; all the killing takes place.

Halloween (2007)

Wednesday, October 31, 1990: We meet the dysfunctional Myers family. Michael's killing ways begin after school and later that night. He is then taken into custody.

September-October, 1991: News reports that Michael is convicted and remanded to Smith's Grove Sanitarium under the care of Dr. Loomis.

1992: Michael kills Nurse Wynn and Deborah Myers commits suicide.

Tuesday, October 30, 2007: Michael breaks out of Smith's Grove, killing a number of guards and other staff members in the process. Gets his new clothes from Big Joe Grizzly.

Wednesday, October 31, 2007: We meet Laurie Strode. All of the babysitting and killing takes place.

Halloween II (2009)

December 1992: Deborah Myers visits Michael and gives him the white horse statue.

Wednesday, October 21, 2007: Laurie is roaming the streets in a daze, carrying Dr. Loomis's gun that she shot Michael with, and covered in blood. Michael escapes the coroner's van after it hits a cow.

Wednesday, October 29, 2008: Laurie has her big nightmare of her time in the hospital two years ago. We find Annie is also still alive. Laurie visits her therapist and heads to work at Uncle Meat's. Dr. Loomis has a press conference that doesn't go so well. Michael is confronted by Floyd and family.

Thursday, October 30, 2008: Dr. Loomis visits the Myers house for an interview. Laurie visits her therapist again. Michael returns to Haddonfield at The Rabbit in Red Lounge.

Friday, October 31, 2008: Dr. Loomis has a book signing, Laurie finds out her true identity and then parties at Phantom Jam. Loomis appears on The Newman Hour. The final scene in the shed on Eagle Road takes place.

KILL INDEX

KILL INDEX

Halloween (1978)

Character	Means of Death	Notes
Killer: Michael Myers (6)		
Judith Myers	Stabbed multiple times	Michael's first kill at age 6 in the original timeline.
Unnamed Phelps Garage Mechanic	Unseen	Michael steals his clothes.
Lester the Wallace's dog	Strangled	Michael also killed an animal of some sort for food in his old house. That animal is not listed here.
Annie Brackett	Choked then throat slit with knife	Michael hides in the backseat of her car and waits for her to get in.
Bob Simms	Choked then stabbed	Michael lifts him while choking then drives a knife into his stomach impaling him to the folding doors in the Wallace kitchen.
Lynda Van Der Klok	Strangled with phone cord	Laurie was on the other end of the line listening to her death.

KILL INDEX

Halloween II (1981)

Character	Means of Death	Notes
Killer: Patrolman #3 (1)		
Ben Tramer	Crushed by police car	The first kill by someone other than Michael Myers in the film franchise. Actually occurred between Alice's and Mr. Garrett's kills below.
Killer: Michael Myers (9)		
Alice	Stabbed in chest	Michael used Mrs. Elrod's knife for this kill
Security Guard Mr. Garrett	Claw hammer to the front of the head	
Budd Scarlotti	Strangled from behind	
Karen Rainey	Drowned in 120+ degree water	Actress Pamela Susan Shoop has said the water was actually freezing and caused an ear infection.
Dr. Mixter	Unseen: Needle in the eyeball	
Janet Newhall	Needle into the temple	
Nurse Alves	Unseen: Strangling indicated, but also cut open and bleeding out	She was in the major surgery room and had an IV in her arm as well.

Jill Franco	Scalpel in the back and lifted a few feet off the ground	
Marshall	Throat slit with a scalpel	

*Jimmy slips on Nurse Alves's blood and hits his head. He later passes out in the car with Laurie. In the TV version, there is a scene with him alive in the ambulance with Laurie.

KILL INDEX

Halloween III: Season of the Witch (1982)

Character	Means of Death	Notes
Killer: Silver Shamrock Robot Henchmen (4)		
Harry Grimbridge	Eyes gouged out, skull pulled apart	
Silver Shamrock Robot Assassin	Self-kill – Pours gasoline on himself and the car and lights himself on fire	
Starker	Head ripped off	
Teddy, Coroner Assistant	Cordless drill into the side of her head	
Killer: Harry Grimbridge (1)		
Silver Shamrock Robot Henchman	Crushed between two cars	
Killer: Dr. Daniel Challis (17)		
Knitting Granny Robot	Shaken until her head falls off	
Silver Shamrock Robot Henchman	Punched in stomach multiple times, wires ripped out	
14 Silver Shamrock Henchmen	Plays the Giveaway and then dumps a case of the Silver Shamrock mask chips down onto a room full of henchmen.	There were definitely 14, but most likely dozens more not seen directly.
Ellie Grimbridge Robot Double	Decapitated with a tire iron	

Killer: Conal Cochran (3)		
Buddy Kupfer, Jr.	Silver Shamrock Mask	
Buddy Kupfer	Swarmed by the snakes and insects that came out of the mask	
Betty Kupfer	Swarmed by the snakes and insects that came out of the mask	
Killer: Various non-humans or unconfirmed (3)		
Marge Gutman	Shot in face with a laser from a Silver Shamrock mask chip	It fried her face.
Conal Cochran	An overload of laser power caused the Stonehenge stone to shoot a laser directly at him. He was incinerated.	Technically, this could be listed with Dr. Challis as the killer, as he set a course of events into action that directly led to this happening
Ellie Grimbridge	Unconfirmed kill, unknown killer – either a robot henchman or Conal Cochran	

KILL INDEX

Halloween 4: The Return of Michael Myers (1988)

Character	Means of Death	Notes
Killer: Michael Myers (18)		
Male paramedic	Head smashed into side of ambulance, thumb through skull	Michael was being transported back to Smith's Grove.
Three other unnamed people in the ambulance	Unseen	Unclear, but there might be one more killed here.
Mechanic	Unseen: Crowbar through torso	
Waitress	Unseen	*The Brady Bunch* actor Mike Lookinland was a production assistant and his wife Kelly portrays the dead waitress.
Sundae	Unseen	The Carruthers family dog
Buddy	Thrown into the transformers	The power worker
Deputy Pierce	Unseen	Shown in the police station
Two more officers	Unseen	
Deputy Logan	Unseen	
Kelly Meeker	Impaled with shotgun and mounted to wall	
Brady	Head squished and choked as lifted	
Three of Earl's posse	Stabbed and thrown from the back of the pickup truck	

Earl Ford	Squished face while driving the pickup truck	Rachel takes the wheel and tosses him out.
Killer: Earl Ford and three of his posse members (1)		
Ted Hollister	Shot repeatedly	They thought he was Michael Myers. This kill actually happens between Deputy Pierce and the two unnamed officers, and Deputy Logan.

KILL INDEX

Halloween 5: The Revenge of Michael Myers (1989)

Character	Means of Death	Notes
Killer: Michael Myers (12)		
Mountain Man		
Rachel Carruthers	Scissors into neck/chest	
Max the dog	Unseen	
Mikey	Three-pronged tool to the top of head	
Spitz	Pitchfork through his back	
Samantha	Decapitated with a sickle	
Deputy Tom Farrah	Unseen, pitchfork	
Deputy Nick Ross		
Tina Williams	Knife into chest	
Dr. Max Hart	Unseen	
Deputy Eddy Grey	Head smashed into steering wheel	Deputy sitting outside the Myers house
Deputy Charlie Bloch	Hung with emergency ladder	
Killer: Man in black (Dr. Wynn) (8)		
Eight Cops	Shot some, the rest killed by explosion	The man in black killed everyone and kidnapped Michael and Jamie.

KILL INDEX

Halloween: The Curse of Michael Myers (1995)

Character	Means of Death	Notes
Killer: Michael Myers (17-19)		
Birthing Nurse	Drives head onto a spike in the wall	
Truck owner	Twists head all the way around	
Jamie Lloyd	Corn Thresher	In an alternative Producer's Cut, Jamie lives well into the film and is ultimately shot by Dr. Wynn while she lay in a hospital bed.
Debra Strode	Unseen, axe to head	All that is seen is the blood splatter.
John Strode	Impaled and mounted to an electrical circuit box	Fried until he explodes.
Barry Simms	Stabbed in stomach from behind	
Tim Strode	Throat slit	
Beth	Stabbed multiple times in the back	
8-10 Doctors (approximate)	Killed in a frenzy complete with strobe effect	Dr. Wynn could have been one of the doctors killed in the theatrical version. In the Producer's Cut, we see him alive after that, but it is assumed he died after transferring the mark of Thorn to Dr. Loomis.

Unnamed Doctor	Killed from behind while running behind Tommy and Kara	

KILL INDEX

Halloween H20: 20 Years Later (1998)

Character	Means of Death	Notes
Killer: Michael Myers (6)		
Jimmy	Ice skate into his head	
Tony	Knife in the back	
Marion Chambers Whetington	Unseen	
Charlie Deveraux	Throat slit	
Sarah Wainthrope	Stabbed multiple times, then hung	
Will Brennan	Knife into back then lifted off the ground	
Killer: Laurie Strode/Keri Tate (1)		
Paramedic dressed as Michael Myers	Decapitated with an axe	

KILL INDEX

Halloween: Resurrection (2002)

Character	Means of Death	Notes
Killer: Michael Myers (10)		
Franklin Munroe	Unseen, decapitated	Guards at Grace Anderson Sanitarium
Willie Haines	Throat slit	
Laurie Strode	Stabbed in back, falls to death	She sort of gave up and let go after kissing Michael goodbye
Charley Albans	Stabbed with leg of tripod	
Bill Woodlake	Stabbed multiple times, then knife into the top of the head	
Donna Chang	Impaled on broken steel rod	
Jenna Danzig	Decapitated with knife	
Jim Morgan	Skull crushed with bare hands	
Rudy Grimes	Mounted to door with three knives	
Nora Winston	Unseen, Hanging and bleeding out	

KILL INDEX

Halloween (2007)

Character	Means of Death	Notes
Killer: Michael Myers (21)		
Elvis the rat	Unseen	
Wesley Rhoades	Beaten to death with a tree branch	Michael's official first human kill in the remake timeline
Ronnie White	Taped down, throat slit, stabbed multiple times in face and chest	
Steve Haley	Beaten to death with an aluminum bat	
Judith Myers	Stabbed 17 times	The first kill my Michael while wearing the traditional mask
Nurse Wynn	Stabbed in the neck with a fork	Perhaps some relation to Dr. Wynn.
Jack Kendall	Unseen, beaten to death	
Noel Kluggs	Head smashed into wall	
Zach Garrett	Hit in head with shackles	In theatrical version only. Some of them can be seen already dead in the Director's Cut. These three and Stan Payne (below) were killed while transporting Michael within Smith's Grove.
Larry Redgrave	Head bashed into wall multiple times	
Patty Frost	Throat ripped out	

Nurse/Receptionist	Unseen, bleeding heavily; unconfirmed death	
Ismael Cruz	TV smashed onto his head	
Big Joe Grizzly	Beaten then stabbed multiple times	Michael killed him for his clothes
Bob Simms	Stabbed and mounted to the wall with knife	
Lynda Van Der Klok	Strangled	
Mason Strode	Knife slash, nearly decapitated	
Cynthia Strode	Neck snapped and stabbed	
Paul	Stabbed in chest	
Officer Lowery	Stabbed in back	
Deputy Charles	Stabbed multiple times in chest	
Suicide (1)		
Deborah Myers	Gunshot to the head	Actually took place between the Nurse Wynn and Jack Kendall kills above
Killer: Patty Frost (1)		
Stan Payne	Shot when Michael uses him as a human shield as Officer Frost fires at him	Actually took place between Larry Redgrave and Patty Frost

KILL INDEX

Halloween II (2009)

Character	Means of Death	Notes
Automobile Crash (1)		
Coroner Hooks	Van crashes into a cow.	It seems he died on contact.
Killer: Michael Myers (1)		
Gary Scott	Decapitated with a broken piece of window glass.	He then begins to walk off with his head until he has a vision of his mother and drops it.
Killer: Michael Myers in Laurie's Dream Scene (3)		
Nurse Octavia Daniels	Stabbed multiple times, knife left in the top of her head.	
Unnamed Nurse	Unseen: Mounted to a stair railing gate, her eyes missing, and the top of her head cut wide open.	
Buddy	Axe in the back.	
Killer: Michael Myers (13)		
Floyd	Mounted on deer antlers on the front of his own truck	Floyd is the father of at least Jazlean
Sherman Benny	Stabbed multiple times	It is unclear if Sherman is Jazlean's brother or husband
Jazlean Benny	Stabbed multiple times	
Howard	Head stomped on multiple times	He is then hung inside The Rabbit in Red Lounge
Big Lou Martini	Brutally beaten, major compound fracture to arm, then head smashed into the wall	*Compound Fracture* is the name of a movie starring Tyler Mane and produced by his Mane Entertainment

Misty Snow	Head smashed into a mirror multiple times	
Wolfie	Stabbed from behind while urinating on a tree	
Harley David	Strangled from behind with bare hands	
Deputy Neale	Strangled with a rope	Killed while standing guard outside of the Brackett house
Annie Brackett	Brutally beaten and stabbed	Dies in Laurie's arms
Mya Rockwell	Stabbed multiple times	
Becks	Thrown through windshield of car, car then flipped down a hill	
Dr. Loomis	Stabbed in stomach	In the theatrical release he is slashed and stabbed multiple times
Killer: Group of police (2)		
Michael Myers	Shot many times	In the theatrical release he is stabbed multiple times by Laurie Strode after being shot twice by Sheriff Brackett
Laurie Strode	Shot many times	Only killed in the Unrated Director's Cut

ANSWERS

JESSICA FEENEY

1) b. Tom Kane. He also provided the voice of Dr. Loomis in a short fan film in 2012 titled *Halloween: The Awakening,* which actually tried to tie all of the different timelines together in one.

2) c. Contract dispute and fate of her character. The studio wanted to pay her the same amount she had made for Part 4. She didn't like the idea of her character being killed off so early in the film.

3) a. Having sex

RON MARTIN

1) c. Dangertainment

2) b. Atari 2600

3) a. Jamie Lee Curtis. She was the voice of the operator on the phone as well as the voice announcing the 6PM curfew.

CLINT NARRAMORE

1) c. James T. Kirk. It was a 1975 Captain James T. Kirk mask that was purchased for under two dollars. Due to the budget, the crew had to find a cheap mask. They came back with a Don Post Emmett Kelly smiling clown mask which was deemed too creepy, so they instead went with the Kirk mask with some adjustments to it.

2) a. *Psycho*. Sam Loomis was Marion's secret lover in the film. Marion, of course, was portrayed by Janet Leigh, who is Jamie Lee Curtis's mother.

3) d. Cleveland Browns. The team began the tradition of playing the *Halloween* theme and flashing different images including shots of Michael Myers on the Jumbotron during the 2013 NFL season.

JOHN CATHELINE

1) b. Row 18, Plot 20

2) c. *Laser Man, Neutron Man, Tarantula Man*. *Howard the Duck* comics were used in the scene.

3) a. Parts 1, 5, and 6. Dr. Wynn was in a scene added for the television broadcast of the original film. He can be seen walking Dr. Loomis to his car. In Part 5, he is the man in black. In Part 6, he is the main villain, apart from Michael.

LUKE SMALUK

1) b. John Carpenter

2) d. Ellie Cornell. In the roof scene, she got caught on a nail as she slid down, cutting her stomach. She wanted to continue filming but they stopped to let her get treated.

3) a. Tyler Mane and George P. Wilbur. Wilbur portrayed Michael in both Part 4 and Part 6

TONY PROFFER

1) c. "Don't Fear the Reaper"

2) a. Sequential Circuits Prophet-5 and Prophet-10

3) b. 5/4 time signature. John Carpenter's father is responsible for Carpenter's knowledge of the signature.

JAMES MAXWELL

1) d. Wrench. If you watch it frame by frame, you can clearly see it.

2) b. Red

3) a. 45 Lampkin Lane. The Strode family lived in the old Myers house in *The Curse of Michael Myers*.

KEVIN S. KING

1) d. *The Babysitter Murders*

2) b. 7. It was said at a convention that John Carpenter wore the mask in some scenes but no one knows which ones.

3) c. A Halloween mask, rope, and a couple of knives.

KEVIN'S CHRONOLOGY

Halloween (1978):

1) c. Judith Myers
2) e. Unnamed truck driver
3) a. Lester the dog
4) f. Annie Brackett
5) b. Bob Simms
6) d. Lynda Van Der Klok

Halloween II (1981):

1) h. Alice Martin
2) f. Ben Tramer
3) d. Mr. Garrett
4) a. Budd Scarlotti
5) j. Karen Rainey
6) e. Dr. Frederick Mixter
7) i. Janet Newhall
8) g. Nurse Virginia Alves
9) b. Jill Franco
10) c. Marshall

I'M YOUR BOOGEYMAN

1) Deborah

2) 6

3) 10

4) The Curse of Thorn

5) Samhain

6) Clown

7) c. October 19, 1957. This is the same year that Jason Voorhees drowns at Camp Crystal Lake in the *Friday the 13th* movie franchise. In talking with writer Victor Miller, I learned it was a total coincidence.

8) d. Audrey. In *Halloween 4: The Return of Michael Myers,* his middle initial is shown as "M" on the transfer form that Dr. Hoffman is typing up.

9) c. Salem Witch Trials. Cotton Mather used the term "shape" to describe the spirits of the accused doing mischief or harming another person during the Salem Witch Trials.

10) a. "Die." Said in the Director's Cut of *Halloween II* (2009) as he killed Dr. Loomis.

11) b. Judith Myers

12) c. Tree branch

13) c. Big Joe Grizzly

PARENTS JUST DON'T UNDERSTAND

1) b. The Rabbit in Red
2) b. Peter
3) a. Edith
4) b. Car crash
5) a. Gunshot

BACK HOME AGAIN

1) c. 1883
2) a. Huskies
3) c. 1989
4) d. Livingston County

#SLASHTAGS

1) d. *Halloween 4: The Return of Michael Myers*
2) g. *Halloween H20: 20 Years Later*
3) i. *Halloween (2007)*
4) b. *Halloween II (1981)*
5) a. *Halloween (1978)*
6) e. *Halloween 5: The Revenge of Michael Myers*
7) h. *Halloween: Resurrection*
8) c. *Halloween III: Season of the Witch*
9) j. *Halloween II (2009)*
10) f. *Halloween: the Curse of Michael Myers*

SOME FOLKS

1) Earl Ford

2) Will Brennan

3) Freddie Harris

4) Ismael Cruz

5) Connor Cochran

6) Nora

7) c. Bucky

8) a. Claudia and Casey

9) d. Lindsey. This was supposed to be Lindsey Wallace, the girl that Annie Brackett and Laurie Strode babysat in the original *Halloween*, but then they didn't expand on her story.

10) b. Principal Chambers

11) a. Harry Grimbridge

12) c. Harold

13) a. Chester Chesterfield

14) c. Linda

15) b. Big Lou Martini

16) d. Mark

17) c. Buddy Kupfer

18) a. Uncle Seymour Coffins

19) b. Brady

PSYCHO KILLER

1) i. Tyler Mane

2) l. George P. Wilbur

3) a. Debra Hill

4) d. Tom Morga

5) k. Tommy Lee Wallace

6) g. Brad Loree. He was actually the first person interviewed for the part and got it.

7) c. Dick Warlock

8) e. Don Shanks. Was also a Santa climbing in a window in *Silent Night, Deadly Night*.

9) h. Daeg Faerch

10) j. James Winburn

11) f. Chris Durand

12) b. Nick Castle

13) m. A. Michael Lerner

THE REAL ME

1) Tyler Mane

2) Tom Morga

3) Erin Moran

4) Hancock

5) c. Sabretooth

6) a. Golden Grahams

7) b. Compound Fracture

LAURIE (STRANGE THINGS HAPPEN)

1) Angel
2) Keri Tate
3) a. Butterfly
4) d. Knitting Needle
5) c. Mason and Cynthia
6) a. The McKenzies' house
7) b. Annie Brackett
8) c. Uncle Meat's Java Hole
9) a. Kisses him
10) d. Headmistress
11) c. White horse
12) b. Chemistry

THE WHICH DOCTOR?

1) e. Dr. Mixter
2) c. Dr. Wynn
3) h. Dr. Koplensen
4) d. Dr. Barbara Collier
5) b. Dr. Max Hart
6) a. Dr. Bonham
7) f. Dr. Daniel Challis
8) g. Dr. Hoffman

THE DEVIL AND I

1) Six times. In the flashback scenes at the start of *Halloween II* (1981), he mysteriously shoots him a seventh time.

2) Lynda Van Der Klok

3) *60 Minutes*

4) 5

5) *The Devil's Eyes - The Story of Michael Myers*

6) c. .357 Magnum

7) b. "Chett, The Bringer of Death"

8) d. *The Newman Hour*

9) c. Reverend Jackson P. Sayer

10) d. *The Devil Walks Among Us*

11) a.Vera. He quotes her as saying, "Freaks will always find their way home."

12) d. Jennifer Hill

13) d. Frederick

14) a. Stroke. Dr. Loomis tells Dr. Wynn during their extended conversation in the Producer's Cut of *Halloween: The Curse of Michael Myers*.

THE MASTER OF HORROR

1) *The Fog*

2) *The Eyes of Laura Mars*

3) Adrienne Barbeau

4) d. Burt Lancaster. Burt's son Bill Lancaster wrote the screenplay.

5) d. *Masters of Horror*

6) a. Danielle Panabaker

7) a. The Coupe de Villes

8) c. *They Live*

9) d. *Memoirs of an Invisible Man*

10) a. Dan O'Bannon

11) d. *Zoo*

12) b. *The Thing*

COME TOGETHER

1) Tommy Lee Wallace. The sequel, *Vampires: Los Muertos,* starred Jon Bon Jovi

2) *The Last Starfighter*

3) *Dark Shadows*

4) b. *Dead Calling*

5) a. *Zone of the Dead*

6) b. *Stake Land*

7) d. *Police Academy*

8) c. Hugh Hefner

9) b. *Daddy and Them*

10) c. *Fantasy Island*

11) d. *Lethal Weapon*

A SPOOKY LITTLE GIRL LIKE YOU

1) d. The Carruthers family

2) a. Goblin Costume Pageant

3) c. Running a bath

4) d. Uncle Boogeyman

5) a. Corn thresher

6) d. Dr. Terence Wynn

7) b. J.C. Brandy

TRICK OR TREAT

1) c. Astronaut
2) d. Harley David
3) b. Princess
4) c. Pirate
5) Jack-o-lantern
6) Skull
7) a. Dead Little Red Riding Hood
8) d. Vincent Vega and Jules Winnfield
9) b. *M.A.S.K.*'s Matt Trakker, Frankenstein, Penguin
10) c. The Rocky Horror Picture Show

MONSTER MATCH-UP

1) i. Pirate
2) k. Magenta – a Domestic
3) d. Silver Shamrock Witch
4) j. Queen of Sheba
5) h. Clown
6) b/c. Frankenstein
7) f. Slutty Devil
8) g. Bride of Frankenstein
9) b/c. Frankenstein
10) e. Slutty Vampire
11) a. Silver Shamrock Skull

SWEET LITTLE SISTER

1) c. 15. She was born on November 10, 1947 and killed on October 31, 1963.

2) b. 8 times

3) c. 17 times

4) a. A few minutes after 10:00P.M. The pendulum clock seen on the living room wall chimes ten times as Michael climbs the stairs to his sister's room.

5) c. Margaret

6) d. Danny

7) b. Steven Haley

SCREAMING IN THE NIGHT

1) *The Fog*

2) *Operation: Petticoat*

3) c. *Anything But Love*

4) a. *This is Spinal Tap*

5) a. L'eggs Pantyhose

6) c. Baroness Haden-Guest of Saling in the County of Essex

7) c. Disposable diaper with a baby wipe pocket

8) a. *The Star Quilt*

PRIMAL SCREAM

1) c. Ophelia
2) b. Samantha Ryan
3) g. Queen Camilla
4) i. Alana
5) e. Aunt Viv
6) d. Dean Cathy Munsch
7) j. Tess Coleman
8) f. Kim
9) a. Helen Tasker
10) h. Wanda Gershwitz

THE INVISIBLE MAN

1) Ben Tramer. He was later seen in *Halloween II* (1981) when he was killed after being hit by a police car.

2) Paul

3) d. Shirl

4) a. Aunt Ruby

5) c. Susan Pierce

6) d. Mr. Casey

7) c. Ted Hollister

8) a. Mark

9) d. Mr. LeClare

10) d. Scott Todd

11) d. Governor of Illinois. Dr. Rogers, who was in charge at Smith's Grove, called in a favor.

12) b. Minnie Blankenship

13) c. The Fallbrooks family's house

DREAM POLICE

1) b. Buddy
2) e. Charlie Bloch
3) a. Lee Brackett
4) h. Ronny
5) c. Deputy Pierce
6) g. Mr. Garrett
7) d. Willie
8) i. Ben Meeker
9) f. Patrolman #3

DOCTOR, DOCTOR

1) *Dracula*
2) *Sgt. Pepper's Lonely Hearts Club Band*
3) *The Twilight Zone*
4) c. *You Only Live Twice*
5) b. Wilford Brimley
6) c. *Innocent Bystanders* and d. *Prince of Darkness.* The first was done well before *Halloween,* back in 1972. The second was a post-*Halloween* John Carpenter film.
7) b. *Great Aunt Tilly*
8) d. *Escape to Witch Mountain*

THINGS THAT MAKE YOU GO HMMM

1) d. Mitt Romney

2) b. Clown College. In 1997 he attended Ringling Bros. and Barnum Bailey Circus Clown College on a full scholarship. He then traveled professionally with the circus.

3) d. Rabbi

4) b. Pauley Perrette. Odder fact: J.C.'s brother, Adam, who is an award-winning makeup artist, did makeup on an episode of *Buffy the Vampire Slayer* titled "Halloween."

DIE, DIE MY DARLING

1) b. Phone cord

2) c. Jack-o-lantern

3) a. Fork

4) d. Ice skate

5) b. Alice

6) d. Steve

7) d. Ben Tramer

8) c. Bucky

9) a. Emergency ladder

10) c. Television

11) b. A paramedic

12) c. Harry Grimbridge

13) b. Samantha

14) a. Wesley Rhoades

CELLULOID HEROES

1) c. *The Thing From Another Planet* (1951) - John Carpenter would go on to direct the 1982 remake of the film, *The Thing.*

2) b. *White Zombie* (1932)

3) e. *Night of the Living Dead* (1968)

4) d. *Plan 9 from Outer Space* (1959)

5) g. *Scream 2* (1997)

6) f. *Halloween* (1978)

7) a. *Phantom of the Opera* (19325)

DEAD MAN'S PARTY

1) d. Tower Farm

2) a. Phantom Jam

3) c. Mickey Stearns

4) b. Barry Simms

BEHIND THE SCENES

1) John Carpenter

2) *Halloween 5: The Revenge of Michael Myers*

3) d. $8000

4) c. Brittany

5) b. Wendy Kaplan

6) c. Paper leaves - They had to paint them the desired fall colors. With such a tight budget they actually gathered them up after each scene so they could be used repeatedly.

7) b. *Halloween: Resurrection*

8) b. Orange Juice

9) a. The Bowling Green Philharmonic

10) a. Jamie Lee Curtis and Scout Taylor-Compton.
P.J. Soles, Nancy Keyes, and Kristina Klebe were all
28, while Danielle Harris was 30.

11) b. *Halloween 666: The Origin of Michael Myers*

12) d. Nancy (Loomis) Keyes

13) c. Tommy Lee Wallace

14) b. $20,000

15) a. *Look Who's Talking*

16) d. Wig. Since Part 2 was a continuation of the
same day, she needed to lengthen her now-short hair
style.

17) c. *Assault on Precinct 13*

18) c. Distributor of *Assault on Precinct 13*

19) c. *Halloween 7: The Revenge of Laurie Strode*

20) d. *Halloween H20: 20 Years Later*

21) c. Dr. Pepper

22) b. Coca-Cola

THE KIDS AREN'T ALRIGHT

1) b. Tommy Doyle
2) d. Lindsey Wallace
3) b. Danny Strode
4) c. Steven
5) b. Lonnie Elamb
6) d. Bit into a razor blade
7) a. Billy Hill

A WHISPER TO A SCREAM

1) *Roseanne*
2) *The Wild Thornberrys*
3) *The Last Boy Scout*
4) d. Five Finger Death Punch
5) b. *Urban Legend*
6) c. Hollywood Ghost Hunters
7) d. *The Legend of Mary Hatchet*
8) b. *Stake Land*
9) c. *Prank*
10) b. *Last Steps*
11) a. *Among Friends*
12) d. Monarchs
13) c. Katherine Heigl

SILENT SCREAM

1) c. *Hatchet II*
2) e. *See No Evil 2*
3) h. *Daylight*
4) d. *Marked for Death*
5) i. *Don't Tell Mom the Babysitter's Dead*
6) b. *Camp Dread*
7) a. *Ghost of Goodnight Lane*
8) g. *Cyrus: Mind of a Serial Killer*
9) j. *The Black Waters of Echo's Pond*
10) f. *Killer Bud*

PAC-MAN FEVER

1) d. 675
2) a. 3
3) b. Jack-o-lantern
4) c. Character was decapitated. After decapitation, two spurts of blood came from the character's neck.
5) d. He ran away.
6) a. A piece of tape with "Halloween" written on it in marker.
7) a. The *Halloween* theme music played.

DOWN ON THE CORNER

1) Smith's Grove

2) b. Reservoir Road

3) d. Langdon

4) c. Floyd Street

5) c. Mill Creek

6) a. Marion Whetington. Formerly Marion Chambers, Dr. Loomis's nurse in the original film. Actually portrayed by the same actress as well.

7) d. Eaton and Chicago. Eaton was 59 miles away, Chicago was 320 miles away, and Haddonfield was 119 miles away.

8) c. Eagle Road

9) b. Smith's Grove Sanitarium

10) 15 Cherrywood

SLEEPING WITH THE TELEVISION ON

1) d. Sgt. Pepper, i. *China Beach*
2) f. Leslie Burton, vii. *Undateable*
3) g. Jackie Ames, x. *The Fresh Prince of Bel-Air*
4) a. Lt. Harding Welsh, iv. *Due South*
5) e. Cassidy Bridges, viii. *Nash Bridges*
6) j. Candy Man, ii. *Happy Days*
7) i. Dauber Dybinski, iii. *Coach*
8) c. Cheyenne Phillips, vi. *Renegade*
9) h. Monroe, v. *Grimm*
10) b. Digger, ix. *John Doe*

GOING BACK TO CALI

1) c. Ronny
2) b. 1922
3) a. Yosemite
4) c. 2 Months
5) d. Ronny. The bullet just grazed his head.
6) a. Corkscrew
7) a. Summer Glen
8) c. Writer of erotic fiction. LL Cool J, who portrayed Ronny, is a rapper, plays a federal agent on *N.C.I.S.: Los Angeles*, and is the host of the TV show *Lip Sync Battle*.

PUT YOUR DEATH MASK ON

1) $1.98. Tommy Lee Wallace did the work to transform it from Captain Kirk to the Michael Myers mask seen in the film.

2) It was the same mask from the original, repainted.

3) Dick Warlock

4) Don Post

5) Jack-o-lantern

6) Ronald Reagan

7) c. Emmett Kelly

8) d. *Halloween H20: 20 Years Later*

BAD MEDICINE

1) d. Nurse Wells

2) a. Jimmy and Budd

3) b. $100

4) b. Virginia Alves, RN

5) c. Jill Franco, RN

6) d. Karen Rainey, RN

7) a. Dr. Koplenson and Morgan Walker

THE WILD AND THE YOUNG

1) c. Samantha and Spitz

2) a. Sarah and Charlie

3) g. Lynda and Bob

4) h. Tim and Beth

5) f. Lawrence and Tonya

6) k. Tina and Mikey

7) d. Molly and John

8) i. Jamie and Billy

9) e. Sara and Myles

10) b. Karen and Budd

11) j. Annie and Paul

THEY'RE COMING TO TAKE ME AWAY

1) c. Grace Anderson Sanitarium

2) e. Ridgemont Federal Sanitarium

3) d. Haddonfield Memorial Hospital

4) a. Haddonfield General Hospital

5) b. Smith's Grove Sanitarium

POP LIFE

1) b. *Howard the Duck*

2) b. *Rear Window*

3) a. Spuds MacKenzie, the Bud Light dog.

4) b. Weird Al Yankovic

5) d. Apple iBook

6) a. Tide

7) d. Dairy Queen

8) b. Jolly Time

9) d. Mike Lookinland. Mike was a production assistant on the film.

10) b. *Cool Hand Luke*

11) a. George P. Wilbur. Technically it would have to be twice.

12) a. Dr. Dementia

13) c. *Halloween III: Season of the Witch*. Allen dated Stacey Nelkin (Ellie Grimbridge in Part 3) while she was still a teen.

14) d. Norma. She is portrayed by Janet Leigh, who portrayed Marion in the classic horror film *Psycho*, which featured Norman Bates and his mother Norma.

15) d. *Frankenstein*

16) a. James Ensor

17) c. Palm Pilot

18) c. Lee Marvin

19) c. Austin Powers

20) b. *Carrie*

VALLEY GIRL

1) *Carrie*

2) *The Devil's Rejects*

3) b. Riff Randell

4) c. Pamela Jayne

5) a. *Private Benjamin* and *Stripes*

ROCK 'N' ROLL HIGH SCHOOL

1) d. Hillcrest Academy

2) b. Haddonfield Junior College

3) d. Long Beach State. This is the same school that Steven Spielberg attended.

4) a. Haddonfield University

5) a. 1949

(O, WHAT A) LUCKY MAN

1) c. "Singin' in the Rain"

2) a. Mary Steenburgen

3) b. "Snuff"

4) d. Jack the Ripper

5) b. Captain James T. Kirk

6) c. Ludwig van Beethoven

7) b. Suck

8) a. Sprint

SINGIN' IN THE RAIN

1) d. *31*
2) g. *Suing the Devil*
3) e. *Cat People*
4) i. *Heroes*
5) h. *Easy A*
6) b. *Franklin & Bash*
7) a. *Star Trek: Generations*
8) j. *Class of 1999*
9) c. *Fantasy Island*
10) f. *Pinocchio 3000*

DRESSED TO KILL

1) Ace Frehley
2) b. JC Penney
3) b. Barry Kicks Ass
4) d. Black Flag
5) b. Cops Do It By The Book
6) c. Sheri Moon Zombie

WE ARE YOUNG

1) c. *Dark Shadows*

2) b. *Spy Kids*

3) d. Chicago Cubs

4) a. *Psych*

5) b. *The Pretender*

6) d. *Star Trek.* The season one episode was titled "Miri." The Enterprise crew find an Earth-like planet inhabited only by children who, once they enter puberty, contract a fatal disease.

7) c. *Little Man Tate*

8) c. *Bio-Dome*

9) b. *Forrest Gump*

10) a. *Species*

11) c. Bill Engvall

12) d. *Children of the Corn*

DIRTY LAUNDRY

1) b. *Back Talk*

2) a. Holly West

3) c. Robert Monday

4) d. WWAR

5) c. News 18 WPKW

6) a. Barry Simms

I CAN'T LIVE WITHOUT MY RADIO

1) "Mr. Sandman"

2) "Love Hurts"

3) "Nights in White Satin." It is shown twice: once near the beginning of the dream sequence, and once near the end quite some time later. I have wondered if it was done as a joke about the length of the song, as it is 7 minutes and 38 seconds in its original form.

4) b. Creed

5) a. "Don't Fear the Reaper"

6) d. Captain Clegg and The Night Creatures

7) b. "What's Your Name?" by Lynyrd Skynyrd

8) c. "Am I Evil?" by Diamond Head

GOD GAVE ROCK AND ROLL TO YOU II

1) i. "God of Thunder" by KISS

2) e. "Do the Boogaloo" by Quango & Sparky

3) d. "Kick Out the Jams" by MC5

4) g. "Don't Fear the Reaper" by Blue Oyster Cult

5) b. "Baby I'm Yours" by Barbara Lewis

6) h. "Tom Sawyer" by Rush

7) j. "Love Hurts" by Nazareth

8) a. "Only Women Bleed" by Alice Cooper

9) k. "I Just Want to Make Love to You" by Foghat

10) f. "The Things We Do For Love" by 10CC

11) c. "Mr. Sandman" by The Chordettes

I GOT A NAME

1) d. Munchkin
2) a. Cherry Bomb
3) c. Voice Man
4) b. Baby Boo
5) d. Deckard

PHOTOGRAPH

1) b. Alice Cooper
2) d. John Tate
3) b. John F. Kennedy
4) a. Charles Manson
5) a. Abraham Lincoln. There were at least eight different photos of him on the wall.
6) d. Giant Cookies . . . A Real Taste Treat!
7) c. Learn from your parents' mistakes; use birth control!
8) d. Frank Zappa. The poster is often referred to as "Phi Zappa Krappa;" the picture was taken by Robert Davidson in 1967 for an article in the International Times.
9) d. The Butcher of Haddonfield

PET SOUNDS

1) d. Dinosaurs
2) b. Cow
3) a. Elvis

1) e. Tooky
2) d. Lester
3) a. Ivan
4) b. Sundae
5) c. Max

SEASON OF THE WITCH

1) Silver Shamrock Novelties
2) Stonehenge
3) b. San Francisco
4) c. Rose of Shannon Motel
5) b. Gilded Rose
6) c. Santa Mira
7) b. Sticky dwarf toys
8) d. Blue.
9) a. A dairy
10) c. Charlie
11) c. 1887
12) a. Sunday
13) b. 9:00P.M.
14) b. Witch
15) c. George A. Romero

MISERY BUSINESS

1) Strode Realty. It can be seen in front of the Myers house which he is trying to sell, as well as on his car. The car used in the scene was actually director John Carpenter's car.

2) The Rabbit in Red Lounge

3) Vincent Drug. It was also referred to as Discount Mart by Lindsey.

4) Nichol's Hardware

5) b. Dale's Gas Station

6) d. Phelps Garage

7) a. Fastrip

8) c. The Old Town Reader

9) a. Rafferty's

10) c. Lewis Bros. Stages

11) a. Libbey Glass Factory Outlet Store

12) c. Penney's

HE'S BACK
(THE MAN BEHIND THE MASK)

1) Steve Miner. He directed *Halloween H20: 20 Years Later.*

2) *Jason X*

3) d. Tom Morga

4) a. Kyle Labine. He was in *Halloween H20: 20 Years Later* and *Freddy vs. Jason.*

5) b. *The Twilight Zone.* The segments directed by Wes Craven were titled "Chameleon" and "Wordplay."

6) a. Daniel Farrands

7) d. John Carl Buechler

8) b. Louis Lazzara

9) c. Greg Nicotero and Robert Kurtzman

BACK FOR MORE

1) *Invasion of the Body Snatchers*

2) b. *Mama's Family*

3) c. *Prom Night*

4) c. *The Sandlot*

5) a. *The Stand*

6) d. *See No Evil 2*

7) d. The Strode house

8) a. *A Nightmare on Elm Street*

9) d. *The Fog*

10) a. *Dawn of the Dead*

EAT IT

1) d. Mushrooms
2) c. Sugar Rice Pops
3) b. Life
4) d. Jelly sandwich
5) b. Orange juice
6) b. Sticky buns

MOTORIN'

1) g. Rev. Jackson P. Sayer·
2) e. Buddy Kupfer
3) b. Keri Tate
4) f. Bob Simms
5) a. Ellie Grimbridge
6) c. Becks
7) d. Conal Cochran

RIDE ON

1) a. Chevy Malibu

2) d. Yamaha Riva Scooter

3) d. The Shaggin' Wagon

4) a. Dodge Ram

5) c. Green station wagon

6) b. 1976 Ford LTD Station Wagon. It was rented for two weeks. The rental company had no idea it was used in the film.

7) c. 1957 Ford Fairlane 500 Town Sedan. The Fairlane is one step up from the 1957 Ford Custom that Janet Leigh drove in the film *Psycho*.

8) a. White Mitsubishi 3000GT

9) b. 1967 Chevy Camaro

10) c. Film's craft services company

11) c. AMEN

12) d. Bob's Ford Econoline van. While the main vehicles being used by characters had 1978-styled Illinois license plates, many of the background cars still had the distinctive blue and gold California plates used from 1969-1979.

THE OTHER SIDE

1) *Child's Play*

2) Re-*Animator*

3) Phoebe Buffay

4) Starbuck on *Battlestar Galactica*

5) *Goodfellas*

6) *Penny Dreadful*

7) E.R.

8) *Clue*

9) *The Texas Chainsaw Massacre 2*

10) *From Dusk Till Dawn*

11) *Chicago Hope*

12) *April Fool's Day*

13) *The Amityville Horror.* Writer of *Halloween: The Curse of Michael Myers*, Daniel Farrands, is currently working on getting *Amityville: The Reawakening* made.

14) *Jaws: The Revenge*

15) Tyra Banks

16) *Cujo*

17) *Dawn of the Dead*

18) *UHF*

19) *Buffy the Vampire Slayer*

20) b. Beverly Hills

21) c. King Tut

22) b. The Tick. Dolenz voiced Arthur, The Tick's moth sidekick who could fly while in his moth suit. Rob Paulsen (*Animaniacs, Pinky and the Brain*, and

hundreds more) would replace his voice after season one of the show.

23) c. Klingon. He portrayed the character Korax in the episode "The Trouble with Tribbles."

24) c. Jay Leno

25) b. *Rock Paper Dead*

26) d. *Ferris Bueller's Day Off*

27) d. *Friday the 13th*

28) a. *Return of the Living Dead*

29) a. *True Grit*

30) c. *Empire of the Ants*

31) c. Commander William Riker. In the episode "The Icarus Factor," his character comes to prepare his son for a command position on the U.S.S. Aries.

32) a. *Krush Groove*. Lisa Gay Hamilton, who provides the voice for his girlfriend Shirl in *H20*, also made her film debut in *Krush Groove* as Aisha.

33) b. Tamara Glynn

34) c. Frankie Brady

35) b. *The Golden Palace*. He portrayed John "Dr. Johnny Fever" Caravelle on *W.K.R.P.*, Charlie Moore on *Head of the Class*, and Sam Royer on *One Day at a Time*

36) d. *Singled Out*

37) a. *Falcon Crest*

38) d. *Bride of Re-Animator*

39) c. *The Practice*

40) a. *Manhattan*

41) d. *Child's Play*

42) c. *The Exorcist*

43) c. *Reno 911*

44) b. *The District*

45) a. *The Help*

46) b. *Toolbox Murders*

47) c. *Friday the 13ᵗʰ*

48) a. *Robinson Crusoe*

49) d. *The Texas Chainsaw Massacre 2*. She was also in *The Texas Chainsaw Massacre III*, *Stepfather II*, *Leprechaun 3*, *Hatchet III*, and *Speed 2*.

ALWAYS SOMETHING THERE TO REMIND ME

1) Sheriff Leigh Brackett

2) Mixter

3) Raggedy Ann

4) Nurse Marion Chambers. It was where her matchbook was from. Dr. Loomis sees hers and then sees it again in the Phelps Garage truck.

5) Ghost

THE NIGHT OF THE WARLOCK

1) c. *Friday the 13th: A New Beginning*

2) d. Richard Dreyfuss

3) a. *Child's Play*

4) c. Kurt Russell

THE NUMBERS OF THE BEAST

1) b. (311)555-2368

2) c. You Suck - 1-800-968-7825

3) a. 274

4) d. 555-2462

5) b.100 degrees

6) c. #11425

7) b. Room 6

8) c. 35 minutes

9) a. 6-L

10) a. 5

11) c. 17

NONSTOP TO NOWHERE

1) c. Janet Newhall. Her name tag does not indicate that she is an R.N.

2) c. Lynda

3) d. Hockey

4) b. Firetruck

5) c. Iceland and West Germany

6) a. A Mexican wolfman named Danny

7) d. A pumpkin with a black cat in it

8) b. *The Wicker Man*

9) a. *Halloween II.* The incident is actually referred to as the "*Halloween II* Murders." Boyer claimed he had watched the film while using PCP, marijuana, and alcohol.

10) c. Chainsaw

11) a. Wat Chun Lee

12) b. St. Petersburg

13) a. Crazy 8's

14) d. Rake

15) c. Pamela Susan Shoop. It was in *Halloween II* in the hydrotherapy tub. Apparently the water was also ice cold, even though her death was caused by the extreme heat of the water.

16) c. 5 Years

17) b. Judge Masterson. 11 months after Michael killed his sister Judith and others, a reporter for WNKW News 5 reports that he was convicted and remanded to Smith's Grove Sanitarium and that

Judge Masterson has assigned Dr. Loomis to care for him.

18) c. C.I.A. He claimed that once the CIA realized they couldn't control him, they packed him up and shipped him off to space.

19) b. National Guard

20) c. Meat thermometer

21) a. Gave it to an inmate of the sanitarium

22) c. White horse statue

23) c. Stuck in the sister of a family drawing

24) a. She broke her ankle at the ice skating rink

25) c. Ether & oxygen

ALL IN THE FAMILY

1) c. Nick Castle

2) b. Kathleen Kinmont. She would later also marry actor Jere Burns.

3) d. Jason Patric

4) d. Pamela Susan Shoop. Her father, Colonel Clarence A. Shoop, would later become a Two-Star General and Commander-In-Chief of the Air National Guard in California.

5) a. *Chinatown.* Roy also played football at UCLA and in the Canadian Football League.

WORD UP

1) b. Made in Taiwan

2) a. SUCK IT

3) b. SISTER

4) b. The evil child must die!

5) d. He is coming for me.

DIRECTOR'S SLASH

1) Rick Rosenthal, *Halloween II* and *Halloween: Resurrection*

2) *31*

3) *The Omen*

4) b. Dwight H. Little. He also directed an episode of the TV show *Freddy's Nightmares* that same year.

5) c. Adam Arkin

6) d. *The Birds II: Land's End*

7) a. *Amityville II: The Possession* and c. *Fright Night II*

8) b. *Bad Boys*

9) d. *Fringe*

10) c. *C.S.I.: Miami.* They were also joined by *Halloween II* cast members Jeff Daniel Phillips and Katie Eischen.

11) d. Pee-Wee's Playhouse

ADULT EDUCATION

1) The Rabbit in Red Lounge
2) The hydrotherapy pool
3) c. Swank
4) d. Vantage
5) a. Sandy Johnson
6) b. *Femme Fatales*
7) c. Parliaments

CATEGORY SONG TITLES

"I'm Your Boogeyman" - *White Zombie*

"Parents Just Don't Understand" - *DJ Jazzy Jeff &
The Fresh Prince*

"Back Home Again" - *Cinderella*

"Some Folks" - *Alice Cooper*

"Psycho Killer" - *The Talking Heads*

"The Real Me" - *The Who*

"Bend Me, Shape Me" - *The American Breed*

"Laurie (Strange Things Happen)" - *Dickey Lee*

"The Witch Doctor" for The Which Doctor? - *David
Seville & The Chipmunks*

"The Devil and I" - *Slipknot*

"Come Together" - *Aerosmith/Beatles*

"I Want Out" - *Helloween*

"A Spooky Little Girl Like You" - *The Zombies*

"Trick or Treat" - *Fastway*

"Monster Mash" for Monster Match-up – *Bobby
"Boris" Pickett and the Crypt-Kickers*

"Sweet Little Sister" - *Skid Row*

"Comic Book Heroes" - *Rick Springfield*

"Screaming in the Night" - *Krokus*

"Primal Scream" - *Motley Crue*

"Demon Speeding" - *Rob Zombie*

"The Invisible Man" - *Queen*

"For the First Time" - *The Script*

"Dream Police" - *Cheap Trick*

"Doctor, Doctor" - *The Thompson Twins*

"Things That Make You Go Hmmm"- *C + C Music Factory*

"Die, Die My Darling" - *The Misfits/Metallica*

"Celluloid Heroes" - *The Kinks*

"Dead Man's Party" - *Oingo Boingo*

"(She's) Sexy + 17" - *The Stray Cats*

"The Kids Aren't Alright" - *The Offspring*

"A Whisper to a Scream" - *Icicle Works*

"Silent Scream" - *Slayer*

"The Curse" - *Accept/Disturbed*

"Pac-Man Fever" - *Buckner & Garcia*

"Down on the Corner" - *Creedence Clearwater Revival (CCR)*

"Sleeping with the Television On" - *Billy Joel*

"Going Back to Cali" - *LL Cool J*

"Put Your Death Mask On" - *Wednesday 13*

"Bad Medicine" - *Bon Jovi*

"The Wild and the Young" - *Quiet Riot*

"They're Coming to Take Me Away" - *Napoleon XIV*

"Pop Life" - *Prince*

"Valley Girl" - *Frank Zappa*

"Rock N' Roll High School" - *The Ramones*

"(O, What a) Lucky Man" - *Emerson, Lake & Palmer*

"Singin' in the Rain" - *Gene Kelly/Malcolm McDowell*

Dressed to Kill - *KISS* (album title)

"We Are Young" - *Fun.*

"Dirty Laundry" - *Don Henley*

"I Can't Live Without My Radio" - *LL Cool J*

"God Gave Rock N Roll to You II" - *KISS*

"I Got a Name" - *Jim Croce*

"Photograph" - *Def Leppard*

Pet Sounds - *Beach Boys* (album title)

"Season of the Witch" - *Donovan*

"Misery Business" - *Paramore*

"He's Back (The Man Behind the Mask)" - *Alice Cooper*

"Back for More" - *RATT*

"Darkness on the Edge of Town" - *Bruce Springsteen*

"Eat It" - *Weird Al Yankovic*

"Motorin'"- *Night Ranger* (lyric from "Sister Christian")

"Ride On" - *AC/DC*

"The Other Side" - *Aerosmith*

"Always Something There to Remind Me" - *Naked Eyes*

"The Night of the Warlock" - *Doro Pesch (of Warlock)*

"Among the Living" - *Anthrax*

"Indestructible" - *Disturbed*

"The Number of the Beast" for The Numbers of the Beast - *Iron Maiden*

"Heaven and Hell" - *Dio/Black Sabbath*

"Nonstop to Nowhere" - *Faster Pussycat*

"We Are Family" - *Sister Sledge*

"Word Up" - *Cameo*

"Turn the Page" - *Bob Seger & The Silver Bullet Band/Metallica*

"Could've Been" - *Tiffany*

"Adult Education" – *Hall & Oates*

"Release Me" - *Dokken*

"The Final Cut" - *Pink Floyd*

SOURCES

Movies:
Halloween (1978)
Halloween II (1981)
Halloween III: Season of the Witch
Halloween 4: The Return of Michael Myers
Halloween 5: The Revenge of Michael Myers
Halloween: The Curse of Michael Myers
Halloween H20: 20 Years Later
Halloween: Resurrection
Halloween (2007)
Halloween II (2009)
25 Years of Terror
A Nightmare on Elm Street
Bad Boys (1983)
Broadway Danny Rose
Cyrus: Mind of a Serial Killer
Dawn of the Dead
Don't Tell Mom the Babysitter's Dead
Invasion of the Body Snatchers (1956)
Prom Night (2008)
Psycho
See No Evil 2
The Fog
The Sandlot
The Stand

Television:
Mama's Family
The Director's Chair

Websites:
Amazon.com
Google.com Maps
HarperCollins.com
HalloweenComics.com
HollywoodGhostHunters.com
IMDB.com
U.S. Patent Database
Wikipedia.com

Note: The majority of things found on any of the websites listed were confirmed by another source or by personally watching a film or TV show.

Photo Credits:
  Kevin S. King: Jack-o-lantern images, pages 1, 14, 43, 48, 79, 152, 205; mask images, pages 105, 108, 110, 111, 113, 139, 190
  Chris Morgan: Mask images, pages: 108, 109, 112
  Ben Fallaize/Father Phantom Studio: Mask images, pages 111, 112, 113
  handiboy.com: Mask images, pages 71, 109, 113, 126, 175
  Jeff Paskach/Midwest Masks N Mayhem: Mask image, page 111
  Kenny Caperton/The Myers House NC: Replica Myers House image, page 172
  Victor Miller: Victor Miller image, page xxi, back cover
  Matt Wolf of Horrifiction: drawing page: 199

Check out author Gene DeRosa's other book,
6-13 A Friday the 13th Movie Trivia Book
http://tinyurl.com/om5koaw

http://tinyurl.com/nauvxnk

http://zombie7.com/

www.rapw.net

http://tinyurl.com/NewBloodCostumes

WWW.HORRIFICTION.COM.AU

WWW.HORRIFICTION.COM.AU

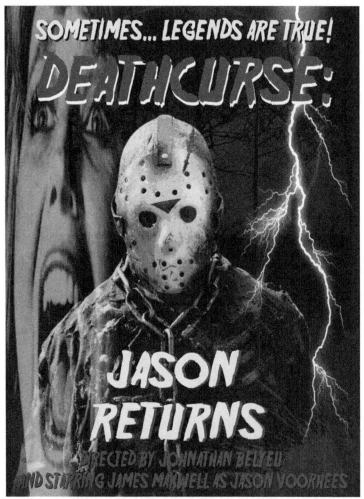

A fan film starring James Maxwell as Jason Voorhees.

http://tinyurl.com/oyv7hyo

GET STARTED NOT SCAMMED
BY LAR PARK LINCOLN

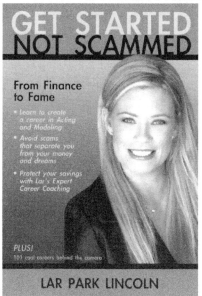

$20.00

(Signed by
Lar Park Lincoln)

Have you been dreaming of a career in acting, but don't know how to get started?

Are you a professional actor who has hit a slump?

Are you getting plenty of acting jobs, but are looking to enhance the quality of the jobs you're booking?

If you answered yes to any of the questions above, this book is for you!

Unfortunately, getting started in the acting business is only half the battle. In "Get Started, Not Scammed; From Finance to Fame", Lar teaches Hollywood hopefuls how to create a career without getting scammed! Learn how to create your dream career by studying with the coach who's been there!

http://tinyurl.com/of8vbqm

Learn how to get started from Lar Park Lincoln, star of:

- *Knots Landing*
- *Friday the 13th Part VII: The New Blood*
- *The Princess Academy*
- and more